We strive to run our company by biblical principles. Our people know that the first goal of our mission statement is to glorify God. *Workplace Grace* gives us a commonsense approach to do just that. I appreciate the teaching, encouragement, practical examples, and challenges that came from reading *Workplace Grace*.

Bern Bertsche
Chairman, Camcraft

Workplace Grace dramatically changed my life and my Christian walk. Now I realize every encounter counts. Although I am a "closer" in business, it is not my responsibility to be the closer every time in my Christian walk. That's the Holy Spirit's job. The unintended consequence has been the more I talk about my faith, the more my own faith grows!

Erin T. Botsford, CFP®, CRPC
Founder and CEO, The Botsford Group

Workplace Grace is one of the few great books on evangelism in the workplace. Every Kingdom-minded employee and employer should use this book as a reminder of our duty and opportunity to love others in our workplaces.

Rick Boxx
President, Integrity Resource Center

Workplace Grace is an excellent tool for those of us who struggle with how to share our faith in hostile secular workplaces. You will be inspired by the material's depth and yet simplicity.

Stephen D. Christensen
Dean of the School of Business, Concordia University Irvine

No faith and work book on the market does a better job of balancing practical advice with theological wisdom. *Workplace Grace* is relevant and challenging for Christians who want to offer their daily lives in service to God.

Marcus Goodyear
Senior Editor, *The High Calling*

Workplace Grace is a guide to being a Christian in the workplace, period. It shows us how to be like Jesus the carpenter in doing our work, relating to others, being sensitive to the moment, and growing close to God. By far, this is the best book yet on living out one's faith in the workplace.

Bill Hendricks
President, The Giftedness Center

Almost everyone I know breaks out in a cold sweat and then retreats when the thought of evangelism comes up. *Workplace Grace* presents a clean, realistic, relational process to sharing life and truth.

Dr. Hal Hadden
Founder and CEO of Christian Leadership Concepts

Workplace Grace articulates better than any other book I have read on how to be an effective witness for Christ in our work. God has called us to vocations, careers, and professions to do His work of evangelizing the world just as surely as He has called pastors, missionaries, and other full-time ministers. Living out our faith in the workplace naturally leads to personal relational evangelism.

Bud McGuire
Principal, Alpha Petroleum Services

Workplace Grace is the best book I've read on how to have a normal conversation about Christ. I recommend it regularly to people in our church no matter where they work.

Bruce Miller
Founder & Senior Pastor, Christ Fellowship, McKinney, Texas
Co-Founder, Center for Church Based Training

Christians who are committed to reaching people through the workplace will find *Workplace Grace* helpful. The authors share practical, commonsense ideas that will enhance your witness to the lost.

Dr. R. Larry Moyer
Founder & CEO, EvanTell

Workplace Grace motivated me to share the gospel and gave me some practical ways to do this in a more God-honoring, organic, and effective way. I am now better equipped for my pastoral vocation.

Tom Nelson
Senior Pastor, Christ Community Church, Leawood, Kansas
Author of *Work Matters*

Integrating faith and work is critical! *Workplace Grace* provides practical how-tos that can have a positive impact in the workplace. A must read for those who truly see their work as their calling.

Diane Paddison, Founder and President of *4wordwomen.org*
Author of *Work, Love, Pray*

I believe this is the best, most thorough and practical resource for marketplace people on engaging others in the context of relational evangelism. I've been personally blessed and challenged by it.

Jonathan Shibley
President, Global Advance

Workplace Grace is a treasure trove of practical application. Every marketplace believer should read this book with expectation. It will transform their understanding of what being an ambassador in the workplace really means.

Lee Truax
President, CBMC USA

Workplace Grace

Workplace Grace

Becoming a
Spiritual Influence at Work

Bill Peel & Walt Larimore

LETOURNEAU
UNIVERSITY
LeTourneau Press

Workplace Grace
Copyright © 2003, 2010, 2014 by William Carr Peel and Walt Larimore
Previously titled *Going Public with Your Faith*
Requests for information should be addressed to:
LeTourneau Press, 2100 S. Mobberly Dr., Longview, Texas 75602

Library of Congress Cataloging-in-Publication Data has been applied for.
Peel, William Carr.
   Workplace grace : becoming a spiritual influence at work / William Carr Peel and Walt Larimore.—2nd ed.

   ISBN 978-0-986479-0-8 (hc)

Cover design: Jody Langley, revised by Jeremy D. Huntsinger and Amanda Battaglia
Interior design: Stephanie Salvatore

To Bill Garrison,

who taught me that most of God's heroes are in the workplace

—Bill Peel

To Bill Judge,

who mentored me in life and faith

and taught me how they work together in the workplace

—Walt Larimore

Contents

Foreword

I have the privilege of leading a unique educational institution. LeTourneau University is consistently ranked on *U.S. News and World Report's* "Best Colleges List," which inspires no small amount of both gratitude and gratification. We also graduate more engineers and aviators than any Christian university in the world.

But nothing sets apart LeTourneau University like our heritage, and that is the point of this book. We were founded, you see, by a businessman. Faith and work are in our DNA.

R.G. LeTourneau invented and manufactured the huge earth-moving machines that helped America's military win WWII. After the war, his inventions built America's interstate highway system. In LeTourneau's mind, all his work was a holy calling. "God is my business partner," he said, and those two passions—faith and work—defined every aspect of his career.

In *Workplace Grace*, you will see how these passions can define every Christian's career. Bill Peel and Walt Larimore call readers to find the holy in their daily calling and see their workplaces as mission fields. *Workplace Grace* brings wonderful new understanding and confidence for living out what you believe between Sundays, whatever your vocation or profession.

This special edition of *Workplace Grace* commemorates the 125th anniversary of R.G. LeTourneau's birth. The university he founded proudly continues his work-faith legacy as we fulfill our mission to claim every workplace in every nation for Jesus Christ.

We hope you will join us.

Dr. Dale Lunsford
President, LeTourneau University
Longview, Texas

Introduction

But you will receive power when the Holy Spirit comes on you;
and you will be my witnesses in Jerusalem, and in all
Judea and Samaria, and to the ends of the earth.

—Acts 1:8

J ust before departing earth, Jesus outlined His strategic plan for spreading the gospel message to the entire planet. First-century disciples embraced this mission and the church experienced immediate growth. Followers of Jesus grew from a few hundred on the day of Pentecost to more than six million by the end of the third century[1]—considerable growth by anyone's calculus.

Fast forward two thousand years. For disciples in the twenty-first century, the marching orders of Jesus have not changed, which begs a question:

Since 75 percent of Americans are looking for meaning in life,[2] and America has almost 340,000 churches[3] lead by more than 600,000 clergy,[4] then,

why is the Christian population in the United States declining while the non-religious population is growing at a rapid rate?[5]

In *Workplace Grace*, you will discover reasons behind this troubling trend and how God wants to use ordinary Christians to reverse it. You will also learn a simple, biblical, historically proven approach to evangelism that does not intimidate Christians or nonbelievers.[6]

You see, religious professionals were not the primary contributors to the exponential growth of the early church. It happened because ordinary men and women took the Great Commission personally and seriously. From dusty Jerusalem streets to soggy outposts in the British Isles, early Christians lived out their faith in bakeries, barracks, barns, and businesses, spreading the gospel with an enthusiasm that could never be produced by wages or sense of duty.

> Evangelism is about relationship. It is a process, not an aggressive encounter.

Day after day, the early Christians gossiped the gospel to friends, relatives, masters, slaves, customers, coworkers, fellow soldiers, and others in their commercial networks. In other words, they took their faith to work.

Workplace Grace is for Christians who want to see coworkers and friends come to faith in Christ, yet they...
- ▶ feel awkward talking to others about Christ.
- ▶ are not sure it is appropriate or ethical to talk about faith at work.

Workplace Grace is for Christians who ...
- ▶ want to know how to make a spiritual difference at work.
- ▶ are not gifted evangelists.

The workplace was the most strategic mission field for first-century believers. Today nothing has changed. Those who are most effective at sharing their faith are ordinary Christians in the workplace who understand that evangelism is first and foremost about building relationships. It is a process, often a long one, not an aggressive encounter or a one-time conversation.

As you will discover, the journey of faith consists of a number of small, incremental decisions. Being part of someone's journey to faith in Jesus can begin with something as simple as having a cup of coffee with a colleague, listening with compassion while a customer vents about a rough week, or going the extra mile for a boss or employee who is under stress.

When you spend time with people and intentionally watch for what the Holy Spirit is doing in their lives, you will begin to see how God can use you in His work of drawing them closer to Jesus, one step at a time. As you read and pray about the principles in *Workplace Grace*, you will discover how in the course of an ordinary day simple acts of service and kind, encouraging words can have a bigger impact than "spiritual interruptions" orchestrated out of a sense of guilt.

> The most strategic mission field in the world is the workplace.

This was our premise in 1995 when we teamed up to develop a course called *The Saline Solution*[7] to teach doctors how to talk about faith with patients. Again and again, doctors who attended our live presentations or watched via video commented,

I feel a load of guilt has been taken off my shoulders.

I never knew sharing my faith could be so simple.

I can do this!

They also suggested that we adapt *The Saline Solution* content for other professions, and that is how *Workplace Grace*[8] was born. Now we hear similar remarks from teachers, engineers, entrepreneurs, and countless others who have learned a new way to think about evangelism and are helping coworkers take one step closer to Jesus.

We pray you will have the same experience.

Chapter 1

Spiritual
Economics

*I've seen far too many Christians who are more than willing
to travel halfway around the world to volunteer for a week in an
orphanage, but who cannot bring themselves to take the personal risk
of sharing Jesus with the coworker who sits day after day in the cubicle
right next to them.*

—Lee Strobel

I n 1921, Franklin Delano Roosevelt was stricken with polio, a
disease he struggled with until his death in April 1945. On the
tenth anniversary of FDR's death, Dr. Jonas Salk announced
that the polio vaccine he had developed was ready for use by
the general public. More than 30 years later, in the late 1980s,
thousands of doses of oral polio vaccine filled shelves in drug company
refrigerators while hundreds of thousands of polio cases were still
being reported around the globe. Supply was plentiful. The problem
was distribution.

Rotary International stepped in and set a lofty goal to eradicate polio
from the world. The organization raised more than $200 million to buy
enough vaccine to meet the entire global need. But they confronted the
same massive problem: distribution. Working in conjunction with the
World Health Organization, Rotarians developed a strategy to identify
the most needy countries and designate "national vaccination days."
Thousands of health officials and volunteers vaccinated entire countries
against polio in a matter of weeks. By 2001, only 500 cases of polio

were reported worldwide. By addressing the problem of distribution, Rotarians saved thousands from premature death or disability.

> Many of the world's problems stem from failure to meet the challenge of distribution.

Supply, demand, and distribution are basic economic principles. A business may have abundant capital, solid management, and quality product, but without distribution, none of it matters. Even with strong demand and abundant supply in the warehouse, if a business cannot get its product to the consumer, demise is inevitable.

Many of the world's problems stem from a failure to meet the challenge of distribution. For example, food production has increased faster than the growth rate of the world's population[1] for the last two decades. In 2013, enough food was produced to feed the entire global population.[1] Yet one person in eight went to bed hungry. A key reason: distribution problems.

THE SPIRITUAL CHALLENGE

The problem of distribution applies to the spiritual realm as well. People are looking as never before for spiritual answers and resources. Things that promised satisfaction (a bigger home, faster car, different spouse) have only disappointed, as they always will, and intensified the thirst for something deeper.

As human solutions continue to fail, more and more people are seeking spiritual help. However, unlike in the past, people are not looking to the church for answers, the former distribution hub for help with life's big problems.

Our spiritual supply chain needs revising.

> Barna Group research released in 2014 reported, "U.S. adults (75 percent) are looking for ways to live a more meaningful life."[2] Barna concluded, "while three-quarters of all adults are looking for ways to live a more meaningful life, 40 percent of unchurched adults say they do not attend because they 'find God elsewhere.'" The search for meaning and answers is strong.[3]

The God of the Bible is a God of *unlimited resources*. The apostle Paul reminded the church in Ephesus that God "is able to do immeasurably more than all we ask or imagine" (Eph. 3:20). God's resources are limitless; His grace and love are endless. Moreover, He longs to pour out this spiritual wealth on desperate and spiritually needy people. Paul wrote to the Christians in Philippi, "God will meet all your needs according to His glorious riches in Christ Jesus" (Phil. 4:19).

The challenge of evangelism in the twenty-first century is not a matter of supply; it is a problem of distribution. The methods used in the past to deliver spiritual aid and assistance are not working. The idea that we can open a distribution center on a street corner and expect those in spiritual need to come to us is not working. In fact, God did not intend for it to work. Instead of a retail business model, He chose one-on-one distribution as the primary method for His followers to dispense His grace.

> The idea that we can open a distribution center on a street corner and expect those in spiritual need to come to us is not working.

GOD'S DISTRIBUTION METHOD

It is a fascinating and humbling fact: the Creator of the universe could have used any method to spread His grace to the world, yet He chose to use ordinary Christians—not a few handpicked superstars—to take His message of salvation to the human race.

> According to a 2013 Barna Group poll, nearly one-third (31 percent) of evangelical Christians (who all believe they should evangelize) have not done so—at least within the past year.[4]

God calls every Christian to be a witness for Him. So for most of us, our mission field is where we spend the bulk of our time: the workplace. Between Sundays, we can be pipelines of God's grace to people who would never darken the door of a church. If that sounds overwhelming, hang on. You will discover how natural being part of God's grand distribution plan can be.

Evangelism Is a Process

Many Christians learned a mechanical, aggressive approach to evangelism. We attended workshops and read books based on techniques developed by people who have the gift of evangelism.

That is the problem. When those of us who are not gifted evangelists muster up the courage to try these techniques, the results are usually disappointing—which makes us feel guilty and often offends others. We begin to think of ourselves as substandard disciples who are simply not able to share our faith. Although we want to see friends and colleagues come to Christ, we stop trying out of fear and frustration.

> According to a 2009 Barna Group survey, since 1995, the proportion of born again adults claiming the gift of evangelism dropped from four percent to one percent.[5]

Most Christians can name a number of people who served as links in the chain of their spiritual journey to Christ.

The problem is one of perspective, not inability. We tend to think of evangelism as an *event*, a point in time when we explain the gospel message and individuals put their faith in Jesus on the spot. Done!

Walt's Experience

As a physician, an aggressive approach to evangelism was uncomfortable for both my patients and me and was largely unfruitful. One day, I quit trying. I figured my practice would just be a secular "tent-making" operation while I carried on ministry in the context of church life. Yet my heart was troubled. Every day I saw 20 to 30 non-believing patients who desperately needed both physical and spiritual healing, but I could not figure out how to meet both needs in an effective and appropriate way.

However, according to the Bible, evangelism is an organic *process*, more like farming than selling. A person's decision to trust Christ is the climactic step, following a series of smaller steps God orchestrates to draw a person to Himself. He typically enlists a number of people with a variety of gifts. Each person plays a different but vital role to help a nonbeliever take one step closer to Jesus.

Bill Kraftson of Search Ministries observes that each Christian in a nonbeliever's journey to faith is like a link in a chain. "It's great to be the last link in the chain," Kraftson says, "but it's not more important than any other link. We just need to make sure we're not the missing link."

The Distribution Process

The Bible consistently uses an agrarian model to explain how God draws a person to Himself. Paul used an agrarian model with the Corinthians to describe their conversion.

> I planted the seed, Apollos watered it, but God made it grow. So neither he who plants nor he who waters is anything, but only God, who makes things grow. The man who plants and the man who waters have one purpose ... (1 Cor. 3:6–8).

Jesus used an agrarian model to explain the process of evangelism to His disciples. He told them they would harvest a field cultivated and planted by others.

> Do you not say, "Four months more and then the harvest"? I tell you, open your eyes and look at the fields! They are ripe for harvest. Even now the reaper draws his wages, even now he harvests the crop for eternal life, so that the sower and the reaper may be glad together. Thus the saying "One sows and another reaps" is true. I sent you to reap what you have not worked for. Others have done the hard work, and you have reaped the benefits of their labor (John 4:35–38).

Jesus also used agrarian terms to explain why some people respond to the word of God while others do not.

21

A farmer went out to sow his seed. As he was scattering the seed, some fell along the path, and the birds came and ate it up. Some fell on rocky places, where it did not have much soil. It sprang up quickly, because the soil was shallow. But when the sun came up, the plants were scorched, and they withered because they had no root. Other seed fell among thorns, which grew up and choked the plants. Still other seed fell on good soil, where it produced a crop— a hundred, sixty or thirty times what was sown (Matt.13:3–8).

- ▶ **The seed:** the message about God's kingdom that falls on soils representing degrees of readiness of the human heart

- ▶ **The path:** a hard, uncultivated heart that cannot receive God's word

- ▶ **Rocky places without much soil:** a partially cultivated heart that receives the message, but life cannot flourish

- ▶ **Thorn-infested soil:** a partially cultivated heart that receives the message, but life cannot flourish

- ▶ **Good soil:** a well-cultivated heart that brings forth an abundant harvest

Jesus' point is clear: A person's journey toward a relationship with Him is a process—sometimes a long one—that involves a number of incremental steps toward faith. Moreover, as with raising a crop, the hard work is required before harvesting.

> Few of us make it in one big decision. Instead, it's a multitude of small choices—mini-decisions that a person makes toward Jesus.
>
> —Jim Petersen
> *Living Proof*

In agrarian evangelism, our job is not to harvest unless the fruit is ripe. Instead, we must discover where the Holy Spirit is already working and join Him at that place..

The following diagram illustrates the various places where we might find people on their spiritual journey toward Christ and offers examples of mini-steps they may take along the way.[6] Note that just as in agriculture there are four phases of evangelism—cultivating, planting, harvesting, and multiplying—each with appropriate activities on our part that match the spiritual needs of non-Christians on their way to faith in Christ and beyond.

Jesus' Guide to Evangelism

Based on the agrarian model, evangelism can be divided into four phases that correspond to a person's journey to faith.

Cultivation: from Cynicism to Curiosity

Possible Steps of Faith

Wary of Christians and truth claims

▼

Views God and faith as irrelevant

▼

Aware that you are a Christian

▼

Recognizes a difference in you

▼

Still has doubts about the Bible but trusts and likes you even though you are a Christian

The Cultivation Phase focuses on softening the soil of the human heart by addressing emotional barriers. The goal of this phase is to break down emotional barriers by earning trust and creating curiosity about our faith. This stage focuses on building relationships and living in a way that piques curiosity, engenders trust, and shows the benefits of being a child of God. This does not mean we must live perfect lives, which we cannot do. It means that we live authentically and honestly, demonstrating to others that we, too, need grace and guidance on a daily basis.

Planting: from Curiosity to Understanding

Possible Steps of Faith

Recognizes difference in you

▼

Looks more positively at the Bible

▼

Recognizes relevance of the Bible

▼

Aware of the gospel

▼

Understands the gospel's implications

The Planting Phase addresses intellectual barriers: misconceptions, misinformation, or ignorance about God, the Bible, or the Christian faith. The goal of this stage is understanding gained through thoughtful conversations, as we plant seeds biblical truth about who Jesus is, what He wants to do for us, and what He wants in response.

As we develop relationships with nonbelievers and they become attracted to what Jesus is doing in us, we can begin to explain the difference Jesus has made in our lives. As curiosity and interest grow, so does appetite for the truth. When people come to grips with spiritual truth, they often begin to see discrepancies between the Bible and their worldview or philosophy of life. They need answers, presented patiently and humbly, to their honest, intellectual questions.

Harvesting: from Understanding to Trust

Possible Steps of Faith

Considers the truth of the gospel
▼
Recognizes personal need of God
▼
Sees Jesus as the answer
▼
Turns from self-trust
▼
Trusts in Jesus

The Harvesting Phase focuses on the will and a person's resistance to trusting Jesus. The goal of this stage is salvation. Even after emotional and intellectual barriers are broken down, the will remains. People cannot feel or think their way into God's kingdom. Ultimately everyone must make a choice.

Our involvement during the Harvesting Phase requires continued conversation, much prayer, and trust in God to draw the person unto Himself, according to His timing. We may have the privilege of being used by God in the spiritual birthing process.

> The longer I am in business, the more passionate I become to be the hands, the feet of Christ. I see so many people who have not known God, don't think about God, don't talk about God. I want to provoke people to at least think about God. I want them to experience the love of Christ through me.
> —Anne Beiler, founder and CEO of Auntie Anne's

Multiplying: from Trust to Reproducing

Possible Steps of Faith

Assimilates God's Word
▼
Joins in Christian community
▼
Chooses to share personal faith
▼
Makes Christ-like choices
▼
Chooses to live by faith

The Multiplying Phase involves helping new believers become faithful disciples. The goal is to help establish them in a community where they can grow, flourish, and learn to lead others to new life in Christ. New Christians need proper care and nourishment in an environment that encourages development toward spiritual maturity.

WHAT IS RIGHT FOR YOUR WORKPLACE?

Living out our faith in the workplace in wise and winsome ways requires that we take into account contemporary cultural attitudes and realities of the workplace in the twenty-first century. People are under pressure; schedules are tight. Every working environment is distinctive; rules and relationships vary between supervisors and subordinates, and between employees and customers.

> As a younger Christian, I was much more aggressive about sharing my faith. Now I'm just trying to be faithful on a day-to-day basis. I'm much more cautious, because the battle is severe, and if it ever becomes known organizationally that you have an agenda, you can get in trouble.
> —Jack Alexander, Chairman and CEO of Geronimo Investments

Each of us must think carefully about the best way to make Christ known in the workplace, given its particular limitations and constraints. Some work environments are hostile toward anything spiritual. Others afford greater freedom and flexibility to discuss spiritual topics. Some are highly scheduled and restrictive (such as the offices of many health professionals) or run on tight deadlines (a media outlet for news, for example), allowing virtually no time for prolonged conversations except after working hours. No matter where we work or how much flexibility we enjoy, being spiritually insensitive is never appropriate.

FIVE METHODS OF EVANGELISM

1. Proclamation Evangelism

This evangelism model features public preaching and announcing the truth to a large audience. Examples are Dwight L. Moody, Charles Spurgeon, Billy Graham, and Luis Palau, among many. John the Baptist, Jesus, Peter, Stephen, and Paul modeled proclamation evangelism in the New Testament. They all preached the gospel to large audiences.

2. Confrontation Evangelism

In this model, a Christian initiates a conversation with an individual (often a stranger) with the goal of leading the person to faith in Jesus. Examples of this evangelism approach include Jesus confronting Nicodemus and the Samaritan woman. Philip's encounter with the Ethiopian eunuch also represents confrontation evangelism. Campus Crusade for Christ (now Cru) and Evangelism Explosion popularized this model in the 1960s.

> When Christians who are not gifted evangelists try to use the confrontational model, the outcome is seldom positive— unless God has already cultivated the heart to receive the gospel.

When Christians who are not gifted evangelists use a confrontational model, the outcome is seldom positive— unless God has already cultivated the heart to receive the gospel.

3. Intentional Evangelism

Intentional evangelism centers on creating opportunities that expose people to Jesus in a nonreligious, nonthreatening atmosphere. It is what Matthew (Levi) did when he became a follower of Jesus. Instead of inviting his friends to the synagogue, he asked them to his home for dinner.

In this model, someone might host an event that creates curiosity, without causing nonbelieving friends to feel ambushed. The event is more about sparking interest than making immediate converts. Such an event might feature a speaker of interest to nonbelievers, or it could be a forum that centers on discussing questions about God or Christianity. Search Ministries and the Alpha course have had tremendous success with this method.

4. Passive Evangelism

This evangelism approach uses symbols, objects, or art to arouse curiosity. Christians hope nonbelievers will notice religious art, Christian magazines, or Bibles that are conspicuously placed and ask a question about God.

The Old Testament is full of symbols intended to create curiosity, and many aspects of the Jewish ceremonial law were designed to draw people toward asking questions. The temple in Jerusalem was a giant symbol designed to teach people how to approach God. In passive evangelism, the symbol says something even when you are absent or silent.

5. Relational Evangelism

This model of evangelism builds bridges of friendship with nonbelievers and measures success by helping people take steps toward Jesus. This was the key strategy of the early church. According to Church Growth, Inc., relationships are still the way most people come to Christ in America.[7]

> Fourteen thousand people were asked: "What or who was responsible for your coming to Christ and your church?" Eight responses were rated as follows:[8]
>
> | | |
> |---|---|
> | A special need drew them | 1–2 percent |
> | They just walked in | 2–3 percent |
> | A pastor | 5–6 percent |
> | Church visitation | 1–2 percent |
> | Sunday school | 4–5 percent |
> | Evangelistic crusade or television show | 0.5 percent |
> | A church program | 2–3 percent |
> | A friend/relative | 75–90 percent |

OUR ROLE

When we become part of God's family, we join His process of drawing people to Himself. For most of us, this will not involve preaching to large groups or aggressively talking to strangers about Jesus. Instead, our job will focus on *cultivation*, building meaningful relationships with people over time, doing what Jesus called "the hard work," fulfilling our role in the Great Commission.

The Bottom Line

Evangelism is a process, not an event. God has gifted each of us to play a critical role in drawing people to Himself. Our job is to discover where the Holy Spirit is working in a person's life and join Him there.

Chapter 2

Called to the Workplace

Let every man abide in the calling wherein he is called and his work will be as sacred as the work of the ministry. It is not what a man does that determines whether his work is sacred or secular, it is why he does it.
—A.W. Tozer

Many Christians see a distinct spiritual difference between their work and the work of their pastor. They believe pastors and other full-time ministry professionals are God's heroes and have a higher calling. However, at least three-fourths of the Bible's heroes worked at "secular" jobs. For example:

► Abraham, father of the Jewish nation, was a rancher who followed God west and built an open range livestock empire.

► Joseph rose to a top governmental position in a foreign country and saved the Near East from famine by savvy trading in grain futures.

► Daniel was chief adviser to several kings and a political leader who worked well into his eighties.

► David was a shepherd, then a professional soldier, and later the ruler of his country.

► Nehemiah, key advisor to a king, took on a huge urban rehabilitation project.

Did these individuals miss God's best by wasting time in secular pursuits? If so, then Jesus spent close to 90 percent of His earthly life wasting time working in a small business—wielding a saw, hammer, and chisel.

Walt's Experience

Before he became my patient, Tom had grown a start-up business into a successful enterprise and developed an outstanding reputation in the community. He also saw several employees and customers come to Christ.

Over time, after listening to sermons and advice from friends, Tom came to believe that his work was secular and he should pursue a higher calling. He sold his business and accepted an administrative role at a mission organization.

Two years later, he displayed an array of physical symptoms. As I got to know Tom and studied his medical tests, I became convinced he was suffering from anxiety and depression.

His symptoms responded well to medication, but the root of the problem had to be addressed. During a checkup I asked, "Tom, do you think you're doing what God wants you to do?"

He teared up and gazed out the window. "Doc, I think God had me right where he wanted me when I was in business."

On Sundays, countless Christians walk out of church buildings and see no connection between their faith and their work. The next six days between Sundays seem like a spiritual black hole with little or no spiritual meaning.

THE SACREDNESS OF THE SECULAR

MYTH
God values activities such as evangelism, Bible study, and prayer more than technology, politics, and economics.

The erroneous belief that sacred work is superior to secular pursuits evolved from Greek philosophy. The Greeks viewed work as a curse, forced upon us by physical existence. People of affluence devoted themselves to pursuits of the mind, such as religion and philosophy, and delegated work involving physical matters to slaves. This view of reality crystallized into Gnosticism, dividing the material realm (evil) from the spiritual realm (good).

Most Eastern and Western religions see the physical world as sordid, in some way unclean, and beneath the dignity of enlightened people. This secular-versus-sacred worldview has plagued the church for centuries and fostered the widespread conviction that work is a major distraction to spiritual development. As a result, many experience a gap between Sunday and Monday.

CONSEQUENCES OF FAULTY THINKING

A secular-versus-sacred worldview has had a disastrous impact on Christians in the workplace and on the church's vision of ministry. British writer and Christian apologist Dorothy Sayers said we should not be surprised.

> In nothing has the church so lost her hold on reality as in her failure to understand and respect the secular vocation. She has allowed work and religion to become separate departments, and is astonished to find that, as a result, the secular work of the world is turned to purely selfish and destructive ends, and that the greater part of the world's intelligent workers have become irreligious, or at least, uninterested in religion.
> —Dorothy Sayers, "Why Work?"

Impact on Individual Christians

Separating the sacred from the secular has affected Christians in at least five ways.

1. We think our work has little or no value to God.

Many Christians wonder, *Am I wasting time on temporal pursuits? Should I spend more time on what really matters to God?* This conflict makes it difficult, if not impossible, to be a dynamic disciple in the workplace.

2. We fail to recognize our spiritual resources at work.

For example, imagine you are invited to:

- ► Consult with Jim Collins about a business decision.

- ► Get advice from Warren Buffet about your 401K.

- ► Learn speech-writing secrets from Peggy Noonan.

So, what if these experts were waiting for you daily at work, ready to walk with you through every decision and crisis? You would be foolish to ignore their offers. We make the same mistake when we ignore God's interest and presence in our workplace.

Acknowledging God's interest and presence gives us access to infinite resources. For example:

- ► When faced with difficult decisions, we can ask for His help with confidence because He promised,

   I will lead the blind by ways they have not known, along unfamiliar paths I will guide them. (Isa. 42:16)

- ► When we fear the consequences of refusing an unethical request from our supervisor, we can gain courage by remembering,

   God has said, "Never will I leave you; never will I forsake you." So we say with confidence, "The Lord is my helper; I will not be afraid. What can man do to me?" (Heb. 13:6)

3. We lack motivation to be a faithful disciple.

True or False?

- ► A spectator will work hard to stay in shape even if there's no hope of ever playing in the game.

- ► If the real heroes on the spiritual playing field are religious professionals, ordinary Christians should leave the heavy lifting to them.

► If the highlight of someone's spiritual life is attending church once a week and dropping money in the plate, that individual will be serious about faith the rest of the week.

If you answered False to each, go to the head of the class.

> How can anyone remain interested in a religion which seems to have no concern with nine-tenths of his life?"
>
> —Dorothy Sayers, "Why Work?"

It is hard to be serious about God if we devote the largest measure of our time, talent, treasure, and energy to a part of life in which we think God has no interest.

4. We suppress our spiritual immune system.

Many Christians today do not look much different from their non-Christian coworkers. They talk the same, have the same work habits, compromise on the same issues, and entertain themselves in the same ways. Sometimes the only difference is where they spend an hour or so on Sunday morning.

Compartmentalizing our spiritual life undermines God's authority in vital ways, making us more susceptible to selfishness, greed, and dishonesty. By sheer force of time and focus, the workplace has an overwhelming impact on the human heart. Marketplace values can whittle away at the thin influence a few hours of worship has on our inner being. Good intentions can quickly evaporate under the heat of competition if we are unequipped and unaware of God's interest and personal presence in our work.

When the most powerful, life-altering force in the world—the gospel of Jesus Christ—is left behind at church or at home, workplace values will mold our character.

> The problem for Christians ... is not that their faith is weak, or inadequate. ... But while they have faith, they have also been formed by the larger post-Christian culture, a culture whose habits of life less and less resemble anything like the vision of human flourishing provided by the life of Christ and the witness of scripture.[1]
>
> —James Davison Hunter,
> *To Change the World*

5. We gravitate toward extremes.

We will try to separate ourselves as much as possible from things we define as "worldly" or we will relegate God to activities on one day of the week and devote ourselves to pursuing success as the world defines it the other six days. Trying to live in one world on Sunday and another on Monday is schizophrenic, dishonest, and profoundly crippling.

> Trying to live in one world on Sunday and another on Monday is schizophrenic, dishonest, and profoundly crippling.

profoundly crippling. Neither our work nor our faith will be satisfying.

IMPACT ON THE WORKPLACE

Separating the sacred from the secular has also affected the workplace in devastating ways.

1. Godless values dominate the marketplace and define success.

Without God, greed becomes the shaping force of the marketplace. With disturbing regularity, corporate scandals and investigations punctuate the news.

Drill down and you will discover that three elements define success and drive the insatiable desire for more:

- ▶ **Power.** How many people report to you? How many obey your orders?

► **Prestige.** Who looks up to you and envies your position?

► **Possessions.** Where do you live, where do you vacation, what do you drive?

2. People become objects to use.

In many boardrooms, the question "Will it make money?" trumps "Is it the right thing to do?"

Although it is the practical equivalent of a permission slip to do harm, one phrase has become a marketplace mantra: "It's not personal; it's business." Imagine saying, "It's not personal; it's the Lord's work." We know God's work is very personal because it is about people. The same is true for business. It is all personal.

3. Trust erodes.

Trust is foundational for business, so it is no big leap to see that unethical behavior spells business disaster. Mark Greene, executive director of the London Institute of Contemporary Christianity, commented on the far-reaching consequences.

> Lack of trust "doesn't work for business as a whole and it certainly doesn't work for big business. Here's why: Big business needs investors. And investors make judgments about their investment decisions on the basis of audited accounts. If you can't trust the numbers, you have no basis for making an investment; you might as well buy a lottery ticket. And if people don't invest, business can't invest, and won't expand."[2]

In a Harris Interactive Poll, 70 percent agreed "most people on Wall Street would be willing to break the law if they believed they could make a lot of money and get away with it."[3]

GOD'S PERSPECTIVE OF WORK

A biblical worldview leaves no room for dualistic thinking. Scripture has much to say about how God values work.

God is a worker.

Unlike gods of Greek and Eastern thought, the God of the Bible is actively involved in every aspect of His world. He rolled up His sleeves, so to speak, as He engaged in creation. The words *physical* and *earthy* describe God's work of creation.

> When the LORD God made the earth and the heavens . . . the LORD God formed the man from the dust of the ground and breathed into his nostrils the breath of life, and the man became a living being.
> Now the LORD God had planted a garden in the east, in Eden; and there he put the man he had formed.
>
> —Genesis 2:4, 7–8

> When we work to meet legitimate human needs, we are working for God and God is working through us.

The Hebrew word *melakah*, used to describe God's work, is the same word often used to describe human labor. No wonder God has a high view of the physical world and the work we do in it. The author of Genesis writes, "God saw all that he had made, and it was very good" (Gen. 1:31).

In today's vernacular and occupation classifications, God worked as a ...

- ▶ surveyor
- ▶ creator
- ▶ organizer
- ▶ landscape architect
- ▶ physicist
- ▶ botanist
- ▶ judge
- ▶ tailor

- ▶ analyst
- ▶ artist
- ▶ civil engineer
- ▶ biologist
- ▶ farmer
- ▶ arborist
- ▶ garment designer
- ▶ entrepeneur

- ▶ planner
- ▶ director
- ▶ environmental engineer
- ▶ chemist
- ▶ agronomist
- ▶ teacher
- ▶ tanner
- ▶ inventor

God made us to work.

In Genesis 1, God gave mankind a commission that has come to be known as the Cultural Mandate.

> Be fruitful and increase in number; fill the earth and subdue it. Rule over the fish of the sea and the birds of the air and over every living creature that moves on the ground.
>
> —Genesis 1:28

The Hebrew term translated "fill the earth" in Genesis 1:28 means "bring to full flower," to develop the potential of earth's resources to the fullest.

As Creator, God could have placed Adam and Eve in the midst of a highly developed world with roads, bridges, buildings, technology, and everything needed for modern life as we know it. Instead, He gave us the earth and all its resources, and appointed us stewards, developers, and co-creators with Himself.

When we work to meet legitimate human needs, we are working for God and God is working through us, whether we realize it or not. We have a God-given purpose to steward His creation and contribute to human flourishing. Think of it like this:

- ▶ An administrative assistant is not simply a schedule manager and meeting arranger. This individual is a reflector of God's orderly character and contributor to the smooth functioning of business.

- ▶ A loan processor is not simply a paper pusher. This person is a shelter provider and dream fulfiller, creating places where families can blossom.

- ▶ A sanitation worker is not simply a trash collector. This person is a vital contributor to the community's physical welfare and ability to flourish.

Jesus is Lord of the marketplace.

Though we may forget that God is in our workplace, He is there.

> "There is not a square inch in the whole domain of our human existence over which Christ, who is Sovereign over all, does not cry: 'Mine!'"[4]
>
> —Abraham Kuyper, Dutch theologian and prime minister

Several times in his letters, the apostle Paul reiterates God's claim over the workplace. He is also our Boss.

Our circumstances are different from those of the first century, but the context—the workplace—remains the same.

> Slaves, obey your earthly masters in everything; and do it, not only when their eye is on you and to win their favor, but with sincerity of heart and reverence for the Lord.
>
> Whatever you do, work at it with all your heart, as working for the Lord, not for men, since you know that you will receive an inheritance from the Lord as a reward. It is the Lord Christ you are serving.
>
> —Colossians 3:22–25

All kinds of work matter to God.

Paul's statement—that all work is God's work—must have had a shocking effect on Greek ears: "*Whatever* you do, work at it with all your heart, as working for the Lord" (Col. 3:23, italics added).

> Wherever man may stand, whatever he may do, to whatever he may apply his hand, in agriculture, in commerce, and in industry, or his mind, in the world of art, and science, he is, in whatsoever it may be, constantly standing before the face of his God, he is employed in the service of his God, he has strictly to obey his God, and above all, he has to aim at the glory of his God.[5]
>
> —Abraham Kuyper

Whatever includes an expansive spectrum of activities. To help us understand, Martin Luther suggested we consider just how many types of workers God uses to provide the breakfast we thank Him for each morning.

In the twenty-first century, we have to include a host of workers: farmers, farm workers, truck drivers, bakers, dairy workers, supermarket owners, stockers, shoppers, and cooks. However, we must not forget the engineers and construction workers who built the roads, and the bankers who provided capital to the farmers, bakers, and truckers. Also, what about the attorneys, politicians, and public servants who protect our ability to do business and make it possible for us cooperate with each other?

When we meet legitimate human needs, we are working for God as much as a pastor, missionary, or evangelist.

Work is a way we worship.

When work is done *with reverence for God* and *with all your heart*, it must be recognized for what it is: worship. From the beginning, God expected us to affirm His worth in our work. The fact that some disconnect work and worship does not negate God's intention.

> Paul's words present a significant problem for people who detach work from worship. How can working "*with all your heart*" fit with the Great Commandment?
>
> "Love the Lord your God *with all your heart* and with all your soul and with all your mind."
>
> —Matthew 22:37 (italics added)

If doing our work is a separate department from loving God, then we would have to disobey one command in order to obey the other. On the other hand, if all work is God's work, then working heartily at something with the intention of bringing glory to God can be an act of love for and worship of God as much as singing a hymn or offering a prayer of praise.

Our work should be worthy of Christ.

Work done *as unto the Lord* demands our best. Neither lame lambs nor careless craftsmanship are appropriate offerings to God. Integrity and quality should stamp our work.

The phrase "with sincerity" (Col. 3:22), implies extraordinary ethical transparency. Our English word *sincerity* comes from two Latin words, *sine* and *cera*, together meaning "without wax." In biblical times, the common way to repair a piece of pottery damaged in a kiln was to fill the cracks with wax, in order to deceive the purchaser. The apostle Paul exhorts us to do good work and be honest in all our dealings—no wax in the cracks.

In everything we do, says Paul, we do it as though we are working for the Lord who deserves our best, as do our colleagues and customers.

KINGDOM BUSINESS IN THE WORKPLACE

R.G. LeTourneau dedicated his life to God as a young businessman, but he was conflicted. LeTourneau loved his work; however, he assumed God was calling him to become a missionary to China. He wrestled with God over what most people believe: that going all out for God means going into "full-time ministry" as a preacher, evangelist, or missionary.

> If I had a religion that limped along during the week, and maybe worked only on Sunday, or while you're in church, I don't think I'd be very sold on it. I think I'd turn it in on a new model that worked seven days a week, that would work when I was at church, in my home, or out at the plant. And that is what Christianity does.
> —R.G. LeTourneau

After seeking counsel and prayer, his pastor advised him, "You know Brother LeTourneau, God needs businessmen, as well as preachers and missionaries." LeTourneau responded, "All right, if that's what God wants me to be, I'll try to be His businessman." A 60-year partnership with God began that day.

That partnership led to 300 engineering patents and the creation of enormous earthmoving machines that laid the Interstate highway system and infrastructure of modern America. He also founded LeTourneau University to train engineers and other professionals to follow in his footsteps.

Since God was LeTourneau's partner, the businessman never asked, *How much should I give to God?* Instead, he asked, *How much of God's money should I keep?* As a result, millions of dollars were invested in evangelical causes.

LeTourneau also believed that it is the job of Christians in business to redeem the nation. He challenged laymen to take their place alongside pastors to make faith concrete. He wrote, "The preachers can tell us that Christianity works. ... But unless we businessmen ... testify that Christianity is the driving power of our business, you'll always have doubters claiming that religion is all talk and no production."

God does call some individuals to leave the workplace to be pastors, missionaries, and evangelists, but that is the exception. He wants all Christians to go to work for the same reason they go to church: to worship God and serve others. When these motives characterize our work, people notice.

The Bottom Line

You do not have to leave the workplace to know the joy of being used by God. He can use you right where you are.

Chapter 3

Is Anyone Hungry?

*Evangelism is not salesmanship. It is not urging people, pressing
them, coercing them, overwhelming them, or subduing them.
Evangelism is telling a message.
Evangelism is reporting good news.*
—Richard C. Halverson

Marketing is about understanding potential customers:
what they want and need—and what will motivate
them to buy. Marketing experts say if you want people
to become customers, you need a good product and
three things to tip the scales in your favor.

▶ **Overt benefit.** People must clearly recognize "What is in it for
me?"

▶ **Persuasive credibility.** Claims about the product, as well as the
person making the claims, must be credible.

▶ **Dramatic difference.** People must see the positive difference
your product will bring in comparison to other products on the
market.

The same principle applies to evangelism. We need to know our
customers. The apostle Paul understood this. Consider the market
research he conducted when speaking to people living in Athens.

> While Paul was waiting for them in Athens, he was greatly distressed to see that the city was full of idols. ... Paul then stood up in the meeting of the Areopagus and said: "Men of Athens, I see that in every way you are very religious. For as I walked around and looked carefully at your objects of worship, I even found an altar with this inscription: TO AN UNKNOWN GOD. Now what you worship as something unknown I am going to proclaim to you."
>
> —Acts 17:16, 22-23

Paul did not communicate blindly. He learned what he could about his audience. He took time to understand the Athenians and their culture, and tailored his message accordingly. He describes his marketing philosophy to the Corinthian church.

> Though I am free and belong to no man, I make myself a slave to everyone, to win as many as possible. To the Jews I became like a Jew, to win the Jews. To those under the law I became like one under the law (though I myself am not under the law), so as to win those under the law. To those not having the law I became like one not having the law (though I am not free from God's law but am under Christ's law), so as to win those not having the law. To the weak I became weak, to win the weak. I have become all things to all men so that by all possible means I might save some. I do all this for the sake of the gospel, that I may share in its blessings.
>
> —1 Corinthians 9:19–23

Of course, Paul was not saying that he compromised moral standards for the sake of being accepted. He did not change the content of his message; he just packaged it differently, personalizing it to the particular audience he was addressing at the time.

> Successful marketing is about how you can add value for the other person.[1]

Think of coworkers you want to influence. What do they value? What do they like and dislike? Do they have a sense of need? What are they looking for—if anything—from God? What barriers must you overcome for them to consider God? What communication strategies would be most effective? What kind of person would make Jesus' message most attractive to them?

MARKET REALITIES OF THE TWENTY-FIRST CENTURY

A successful business must stay abreast of current market realities. Likewise, Christians need to understand current cultural realities—both in our country and particular workplace—before broaching spiritual topics with coworkers. We must consider the following factors and tailor our conversations accordingly.

1. Corporate Culture

Several dynamics create the unique atmosphere of every office and job site. Multiple factors impact the working environment in positive or negative ways: age and traditions of the company, mission statement, values of its leaders, and products or services it offers.

In your workplace, how would you describe the attitude of leadership toward spiritual issues? In what ways are employees diverse? How do employees practice political correctness? Is the atmosphere faith-friendly or faith-adverse?

2. Age and Life Stage of Coworkers

Four generations comprise today's workforce: Millennials, GenExers, Boomers, and the Silent Generation. Each generation has different values, experiences, knowledge, cultural familiarity, and preferred methods of communication. These differences are important to consider when building relationships with individuals in generations other than our own. For example, facts and logical

> Each generation has different values, experiences, knowledge, cultural familiarity, and preferred methods of communication.

45

arguments typically resonate with Boomers, but not necessarily with Millennials. GenExers tend to be skeptical. Members of the Silent Generation often feel uncomfortable speaking openly and personally about religion. It is important to know these generational traits.

3. Cultural and Religious Trends

Recent surveys and studies reveal some significant trends and felt needs among American adults.

► Twenty percent described themselves as lonely, and 35 percent said their life is stressed. [2]

► Seventy-seven percent reported they were concerned about the future.[3]

► Seventy-five percent said they are looking for ways to live a more meaningful life.[4]

► More than half (56 percent) stated they believe the Bible has *too little* influence in U.S. society, while thirteen percent believe it has *too much* influence.[5]

> Our culture is being shaken to its core by the seismic shift away from God and religious institutions where people have traditionally looked for answers.

These trends reveal angst about life and the direction of our culture. Our culture is being shaken to its core by the seismic shift away from God and religious institutions where people have traditionally looked for answers. Among American adults:

► One-third do not consider themselves a "religious person."[6]

► Overall church attendance in America dipped from 43 percent in 2004 to 36 percent in 2014.[7]

► Those who say they "seldom" or "never" attend religious services (aside from weddings and funerals) rose from 25 percent in 2003 to 29 percent in 2013.[8]

- One-third of adults under age 30 are religiously unaffiliated as of 2012.[9]

- In 2013, only 74 percent of Americans say they believe in God, an eight percent decline since 2009.[10]

- Forty-four percent say they spend no time seeking "eternal wisdom."[11]

- Forty-six percent say they never wonder whether they will go to heaven.[12]

- Two-thirds say religion is losing its influence in American life.[13]

Given a host of conflicting cultural voices and a hostile media who often portray Christians in a negative light, Christianity does not look like a faith most people can relate to, much less benefit from—unless we show them differently.

> Christianity does not look like a faith most people can relate to, much less benefit from—unless we show them differently.

4. A Pluralistic Society

For 200 years, America was called "the great melting pot." Men and women came from all over the world to settle this land. They left the Old World behind to become Americans. They learned English, and their native languages were all but forgotten by the second generation. These folks were proud of their new identity and adopted new traditions.

America in the twenty-first century is a very different place.
- 55.4 million Americans (20 percent) speak a language other than English in their homes.[14]
- 25.3 million LEP (Limited English Proficient) individuals accounted for approximately nine percent of the total U.S. population ages five and older in 2011.[15]

Today, ethnic and religious diversity has ushered in a variety of faiths and worldviews that compete for recognition. No longer is a Judeo-Christian worldview the only perspective people consider in determining values and understanding life.

However, outside forces are not the only influences that affect culture. Philosophies once confined to elite universities are now considered mainstream. Diverse views of sexuality, family, spirituality, and life itself have made their way into the daily cultural debate as more and more people abandon the Bible as the source of truth and the standard for right and wrong.

> We can no longer assume that people know familiar Bible verses, stories, and characters.

5. Biblical Ignorance

When broaching spiritual topics, we have a different beginning point than we did just a few decades ago. We can no longer assume that people know familiar Bible verses, stories, and characters. In the past, biblical knowledge had a significant impact on communication. The Miracle at Dunkirk illustrates this point.

In the summer of 1940, more than 350,000 soldiers, most of them British, were trapped across the English Channel at Dunkirk. As German forces moved closer and a massacre was almost certain, a British naval officer cabled three words to London: "But if not."

In that day, people were Bible literate. They recognized the three words as those used by Shadrach, Meshach, and Abednego in reference to the fiery furnace, when they were resolved to obey God, whether or not He chose to save them. (Daniel 3:16-18)

British families and fishermen understood the message: Only a miracle would save them, but there would be no surrender. They responded to this desperate call for help with merchant marine boats, pleasure cruisers, and fishing boats, and evacuated the soldiers to safety.

A 2013 American Bible Society survey[16] found that although the Bible continues to be America's undisputed best-seller...

▶ Bible reading and perceptions about the Bible have become increasingly polarized, with six million new Bible antagonists.

▶ Although eighty percent agreed that the Bible is sacred and 66 percent agreed that the Bible contains everything a person needs to know to live a meaningful life, 58 percent say they do not personally want wisdom and advice from the Bible.

6. Postmodern Thinking

Americans, especially those born after 1960, are increasingly postmodern in outlook. The modern era began with the rational, scientific thinking of the Renaissance (fourteenth through seventeenth centuries). Although many view postmodernism as a threat to the Christian faith, it is no more a threat than was modernism—just a different one.

Modernism vs. Postmodernism[17]

Modernism	Postmodernism
Effects have causes	Stuff happens
"The Truth" is attainable	Nothing can be proven
"Truth" is discovered	"Truth" is constructed
Reason is trusted	Objective reason denied
Values facts	Values relationships
Man is a biological machine	Man is a social being
Materialistic	Looking for meaning

A foundational tenet of postmodern thinking is relativism: There is no such thing as absolute truth and no clear line between right and wrong. Truth claims are often viewed as power plays—as one person or group seeks to dominate others. People with a postmodern viewpoint often embrace what has been called *expressive individualism*: "If it works for me, it is true for me."

Postmodern truth, then, is something discoverable from within,

> Our business is to present the Christian faith clothed in modern terms, not to propagate modern thought clothed in Christian terms. Confusion here is fatal.
> —J. I. Packer

not from an outside authority. Based on this premise, no one religion is universally or exclusively true. When applied to the gospel, such thinking undermines the prospect for intelligent and rational dialogue on moral, ethical, and even factual issues. The Bible's claim that Jesus is the *only* way to God is an intolerant perspective in a postmodern world.

Postmodern thinkers view a Christian's insistence that the Bible is God's authoritative word as arrogant and ignorant. They brandish the word *intolerant* on those who say that salvation is obtained only through Christ.

Postmodernists have made great inroads into American thinking by asserting a skewed idea that a *tolerant* person is one who *accepts* all views as equally valid—even if the views contradict each other.

However, according to the Oxford dictionary, tolerance is defined as *"the ability or willingness to tolerate something, in particular the existence of opinions or behavior that one does not necessarily agree with."*[18] Big difference!

Interestingly, postmodern thinkers have no tolerance for people who do not accept all ideas as equally true, while showing no tolerance toward Christianity's view of salvation.

The fact is, Christianity is the most tolerant of all religions. Jesus says we are to love *even our enemies*, no matter what our differences (see Luke 6:27-31). This approach to life goes far beyond what society views as tolerant.

> Christianity is the only faith that has at its heart a man dying for his enemies, forgiving them rather than destroying them. This must be presented to our culture as an unparalleled resource for living in peace in a pluralistic society.[19]
>
> –Tim Keller

Perhaps the most insidious effects of postmodernism are the *cynicism* and *despair* it leaves in its wake. When nothing outside one's self defines the meaning of life, people have no captivating reason for which to live.

> Never worry about numbers. Help one person at a time, and always start with the person nearest you.
>
> —Mother Teresa

Internally defined purpose has no compelling power for people who are disconnected from the Author of meaning and purpose.

Although many postmodernists cynically reject religion as a myth, they hunger for meaning and something that will bring order and purpose to their lives. They find themselves with no treatment for the guilt they experience and no antidote for their lack of satisfaction.

THE CHALLENGE

When we go to work tomorrow as ambassadors for Christ, to whom will we speak? The man in the office next door may be a Pakistani—and perhaps a Muslim. The woman down the hall may be a radical feminist—maybe even an atheist. What do we say? What will cause them to listen long enough to learn how much God loves them and longs to give them abundant life on earth and eternity in His presence? If we do not take the time to understand our audience, doors may slam.

Antagonism toward God is not a modern problem. Throughout history God's people have taken His truth into hostile cities, nations, and workplaces. Though degrees of

> Antagonism toward God is not a modern problem.

adversity and methods for expressing it vary in different ages and places, God never changes. He is superior to and victorious over any strategy the Evil One uses to halt the message of the gospel. No manner of thinking or cultural trend or office environment is too hostile—and no person too hopeless—for the all-sufficient power of God to penetrate.

> They hate the truth for the sake of the object which they love instead of the truth. They love truth for the light it sheds, but hate it when it shows them as being wrong.
>
> —St. Augustine

Whether we see today's environment for evangelism as a fearful challenge or privileged opportunity reveals how much our own worldview has been influenced either by culture or by the Bible. Do we believe that God loves the people with whom we work? Could it be He wants to use us to introduce them to Himself? What will they see in us that could pique their interest in learning about Him?

THE POWER OF RELATIONSHIP

Postmodern thinkers value relationships—a decided advantage for Christians. God is a relational God of love. He gives us the power to love others and opens doors for us to demonstrate His love to our coworkers. A personal relationship with Jesus is a powerful testimony when lived out seven days a week.

> People must not only hear but feel, see, and experience the grace of God we speak about.
>
> —Jim Cymbala

Nonbelievers will take note of our joy when we work, our peace in the midst of disappointment, and our graciousness toward people who try our patience. Like the adage, we may be the only Bible people ever read—at least to this point in their lives.

People will best be able to find Jesus when followers of Jesus bring Jesus to them. This begins by being alert to their interests, recognizing their worldview, accepting them where they are, and in the context of a relationship, showing them what it looks like to be a child of God. Moreover as we do, we join the Holy Spirit in preparing the soil of their heart to receive the seeds of truth in future conversations.

Are people spiritually hungry? Definitely. Can Jesus satisfy their hunger? Absolutely. Does He want to use us to show them where to find bread? That has been His plan from the beginning.

So, how are you doing? On a scale of 1 (desperately need help) to 5 (doing great), how would you score your faith's attractiveness to others?

- ▶ Overt **benefit.** When people observe how you live and work, do they see the benefits of being a child of God?

- ▶ Persuasive **credibility**. Do your actions match your words, attesting to the truth of what you believe?

- ▶ Dramatic **difference**. Do people see that your faith brings a positive difference to your life and work?

No matter how you answered, remember: God could have created a perfect, no-fail strategy to get His message out. Instead, He chose to use sinful, rebellious, broken people to represent Him to the world.

Consider the failures of some God used to carry His message. Abraham was a liar. Jacob a schemer. Samson was a womanizer. David was an adulterer and murderer. Elijah suffered from depression. James and John were self-centered "climbers." Peter denied Jesus to save his own neck, and Paul was a murderer.

When we fail as ambassadors (which we will), we need to remember this truth: Honest, authentic followers of Christ who know the power of God's grace firsthand, earn both the respect of others and God's smile.

The Bottom Line

As Christians, we have what people want. We simply need to communicate in winsome ways they can understand.

Cultivation

Be wise in the way you act toward outsiders;
make the most of every opportunity.
Let your conversation be always full of grace, seasoned with salt,
so that you may know how to answer everyone.
—Colossians 4:5-6

Chapter 4

Earning the Right to Be Heard

Few things are more infectious than a godly lifestyle.
The people you rub shoulders with every day need that kind of challenge.
Not prudish. Not preachy.
Just cracker-jack clean living.
Just honest goodness, bone-deep non-hypocritical integrity.
—Chuck Swindoll

Being Christ's witness to the human race is the work of every believer. Some, however, view their responsibility from one of two extreme vantage points that can disrupt the spiritual distribution process.

Christians who take the words of St. Francis literally are at one end of the spectrum: "Preach the gospel at all times, and when necessary, use words." They use this statement to rationalize their reluctance to talk about their faith with those who need to hear the gospel. They believe that they fulfill Christ's call to be a witness by the way they live, and never explain *why* they live the way they do.

Of course, living in a way that honors and reflects Christ is a vital part of what it means to be a witness. But being a witness also requires words.

> The person who says naively, "I don't preach; I just let my life speak," is insufferably self-righteous. None of us is good enough to witness by our life alone.[1]
>
> —Elton Trueblood,
> *The Company of the Committed*

At the opposite end of the spectrum are over-zealous Christians who create more heat than light, forgetting that people need to see Christ in Christians before hearing how much they need to be one. Words without deeds, as well as deeds without words, are generally ineffective.

WITNESSING VS. BEING A WITNESS

In Acts 1:8 the word *witnesses* is a noun. The emphasis is on *being* a witness, not on *witnessing*. In fact, we are never commanded to *go witnessing* (verb), but to *be witnesses* (noun). Focusing on *doing* before *being* disconnects who we are from what we say.

> When witnessing is a verb, it becomes something we do or don't do. We turn it on or we turn it off. … It's something we are supposed to go out and do, and poor, unsuspecting non-Christians often have to bear the brunt of our spiritual obligation.[2]
>
> —John Fischer,
> *Fearless Faith*

When we *go witnessing (verb)*, we usually know little to nothing about the status of the Holy Spirit's work in the lives of the people we meet. And they know little to nothing about us that gives them a reason to trust what we say. In this context, we challenge people to take a quantum leap of faith, rather than a small step toward Jesus. This can add more rocks on the hard soil of someone's heart.

A Painful Lesson with a Sad Ending

Jim wanted to run the other way when a friend urged him to go on a short-term mission trip. Faith was a private part of Jim's life, so talking to people about Jesus in a foreign country—or anywhere, for that matter—was not appealing in the least. His friend, however, was persistent, and Jim reluctantly agreed to go.

When they arrived in the impoverished Latin American country, they attended a training session about sharing the gospel. Then they divided up into teams of two and walked from house to house with an interpreter. Fascinated by the opportunity to meet Americans, the locals packed out small living quarters and listened to what the visitors had to say.

The spiritual vacuum and difficult economic conditions created a gnawing spiritual hunger in hearts, so when team members took turns sharing their testimony and the gospel, many people trusted Christ on the spot. Jim was astonished and thrilled to be used by God in a way he never dreamed.

At the end of the trip, the entire team celebrated that God had used them to bring more than 100 people into His Kingdom. After praying for their new brothers and sisters in Christ, the team leader reminded the group that people back home were hungry for the gospel too. He challenged them to continue boldly speaking about their faith and expect God to do great things.

Jim returned to work with a new sense of mission. When coworkers asked about his trip, Jim interpreted each inquiry as an open door to share his testimony and the gospel message like he had learned to do on the trip. Response from coworkers, however, was not what Jim expected. Some listened out of courtesy; others tried to avoid him. One even asked, "If faith is the most important thing in your life, why are we just now hearing about it?"

By the end of the week, Jim felt discouraged and embarrassed. He decided unless he is out of the country, he should keep his faith to himself.

Jim, like many Christians, did not understand that evangelism is about more than the message. Consider these guidelines:

How we broach spiritual conversation with nonbelievers should fit the situation.

> With each individual, I try to see where I fit into God's plan for bringing that person to Christ.
> —Larry Moyer

What works on the mission field in another country is often not appropriate in an office in the United States. However, all around the world God is drawing people to Himself in miraculous ways. He is sovereign over all, and He has the right and ability to accomplish whatever, whenever, wherever He desires. And, whenever and wherever He uses us, He wants us to be wise.

> I know that the LORD is great, that our Lord is greater than all gods. The LORD does whatever pleases him, in the heavens and on the earth, in the seas and all their depths.
> —Psalm 135:5-6
>
> ... My purpose will stand, and I will do all that I please. ... What I have said, that will I bring about; what I have planned, that will I do.
> —Isaiah 46:10-11
>
> From a wise mind comes wise speech; the words of the wise are persuasive.
> —Proverbs 16:23 (NLT)

Our job is not so much to bring people to Jesus as it is to bring Jesus to people.

Spiritual influence is about more than zeal to spread the gospel. People need to see and be attracted to Jesus in us before we try to persuade them to trust Him.

Evangelism begins with issues of the heart.

It does not matter if we are skilled at persuasion, adept at apologetics, and have no fear of talking about our faith with strangers, becoming a person of spiritual influence always begins with the heart, not the head.

It does not matter if we are skilled at persuasion, adept at apologetics, and have no fear of talking about our faith with strangers, becoming a person of spiritual influence always begins with the heart, not the head.

ISSUES OF THE HEART

Whether growing acres of wheat or planting a backyard vegetable garden, cultivation is key to a successful harvest. Breaking up the soil, removing rocks, and pulling weeds always comes before planting.

In Matthew 13, Jesus describes the human heart as rough terrain for farming. Weeds, rocks, and hard-packed soil thwart penetration of the seed of Truth. Jesus explained that heart soil also needs preparation. Just as farmers face obstacles that must be removed before they can plant, Christians who want to see eternal life spring up in the lives of coworkers also face obstacles: hearts filled with barriers that must be removed before the seed of faith can take root in the heart and grow into eternal life.

> I am very cautious when I think about evangelism in the workplace because I always ask myself if I have earned the right with this person. Have I demonstrated Christian love in this relationship, and have I earned the right to share Christ with them?
> —Jack Alexander, Chairman and CEO of Geronimo Investments

Soil Analysis

Most nonbelieving adults have significant emotional barriers, issues that have hardened their hearts and trained them to keep spiritual truth at arm's length. Think of emotional barriers—indifference, mistrust, antagonism, or fear toward Christians or Christianity—as negative attitudes that create an aversion to the gospel.

Sometimes, emotional barriers are based on negative experiences with religious groups or Christians who are narrow-minded, judgmental, or fanatical. Even well-intentioned Christians who come on too strong can foster mistrust or anger, and inadvertently "damage the harvest."

> When we Christians behave badly, or fail to behave well, we are making Christianity unbelievable to the outside world. ... Our careless lives set the outer world talking; and we give them grounds for talking in a way that throws doubt on the truth of Christianity.
>
> —C. S. Lewis

The hearts of nonbelievers can also harden when high-profile Christians publically fall. Moral and ethical failure of pastors, priests, business leaders, and community icons have fed the general media narrative that Christianity is a giant hoax and Christians cannot be trusted.

Hypocrisy may have turned more hearts away from Jesus than anything else. Hypocritical family members, neighbors, teachers, and coworkers do incalculable damage to the cause of Christ.

> In 2013, the Barna Group studied hypocrisy in present-day Christianity. Among those who self-identified themselves as Christians, research, based on a list of self-selected attitudes and actions, found that 51 percent described themselves more like Pharisees (hypocritical, self-righteous, judgmental) as opposed to only 14 percent that modeled the actions and attitudes of Jesus (selfless, empathy, love).[3]

Perhaps we should not be surprised when people depict Christians as hypocrites. Joe's story illustrates what hypocrisy leaves in its wake.

Why Joe Left the Church

Joe attended church for the first time when a church bus picked up gang members to take them to a youth service. Joe began attending regularly because he was looking for answers to life's problems his parents and friends couldn't give him. When two deacons got into an ugly public dispute, the church split, hurting many people. That's when Joe stopped attending. The hateful, vindictive behavior of the deacons convinced him that the love he had experienced was only for show. He decided that had no use for Christianity and didn't set foot in a church again for over three decades.

Soil Treatment

What will break through emotional barriers that harden heart soil? Will preaching? Rational arguments? Persuasive words? God can use any method He chooses to cultivate the hearts of nonbelievers and draw them to Himself. Sometimes He uses difficult circumstances to plow hardened hearts. But often He uses those whose own heart soil is softened and fruitful to cultivate the hearts of others. People who reflect Christ's character and demonstrate His love, compassion, integrity, graciousness, and patience.

The Cultivation Phase of evangelism is about earning the right to be a spiritual influence in someone's life. The goal of this phase is to break down emotional barriers by earning trust and creating curiosity about our faith.

Trust is not automatic. It is a response to character and actions. We build trust in many ways, but three in particular stand out: competence in our work, godly character, and concern for others.

I feel responsible to be a spiritual influence in my workplace in many ways. One of them is by being good to the employees and exceeding their expectations. If your light is going to shine, your actions should confirm what you say. If your actions don't confirm what you say, then you confuse those around you.

—Anne Beiler, founder and CEO of Auntie Anne's

ESSENTIALS FOR SPIRITUAL INFLUENCE AT WORK

1. Competence

A foundational requirement for spiritual influence is doing good work. Striving for excellence in our work is not about competition or comparison; it is about doing our personal best.

Scripture speaks about the importance of doing good work in a number of places. For instance:

▶ **Proverbs 22:29:** Do you see a man skilled in his work? He will serve before kings; he will not serve before obscure men.

▶ **Ecclesiastes 9:10:** Whatever your hand finds to do, do it with all your might.

▶ **Colossians 3:23** Whatever you do, work at it with all your heart...

Scripture also provides examples of people whose lives demonstrate the connection between quality work and spiritual influence. Look at the example Daniel set. King Nebuchadnezzar interviewed Daniel and his friends at the end of their training and, "In every matter of wisdom and understanding about which the king questioned them, he found them ten times better than all the magicians and enchanters in his whole kingdom" (Dan.1:20).

If we want people to pay attention to our faith, we must first pay attention to our work.

Seventy years later, King Darius discovered the same extraordinary competence: "Now Daniel so distinguished himself among the administrators and the satraps by his exceptional qualities that the king planned to set him over the whole kingdom" (Dan. 6:3).

Nehemiah is another example of the connection between quality work and spiritual influence. Had he not displayed competence, it is doubtful the king would have appointed him to be cupbearer, putting his life in Nehemiah's hands. Nor would the king have given Nehemiah leave from his position to oversee the gargantuan task of rebuilding the walls around Jerusalem, much less given him the resources to do it (Neh. 2:1-8).

Consider Jesus Himself. Can you imagine Him using substandard materials, doing shoddy carpentry work, or overcharging His customers? If He had done so, customers who heard Jesus teach would have every reason to conclude that His theology was only as reliable as His tables.

2. Character

In addition to doing good work, character is the second prerequisite for spiritual influence. For people to become interested in Jesus, they need to see Jesus in us.

Christ-like character engages attention and invites admiration. Every human being is created in God's image, and we instinctively respect the character traits of the God who designed us— even those who do not know God. We value love, joy, peace, patience, kindness, goodness, faithfulness, gentleness, and self-control.

In Jesus' day, many people were repulsed by the religious leaders; however, they were attracted to Jesus because He embodied those characteristics.

> How do you convince a world that God is alive? By His aliveness in your life, by His work in producing reality in your experience.
> —Howard Hendricks

When we receive God's gift of eternal life, He begins the process of transforming us into the image of Christ. Paul writes, "For those God foreknew he also predestined to be conformed to the likeness of his Son..." (Rom. 8:29).

As we spend time with Him, growing in grace and knowledge of His truth, Christ's character begins to replace our old character. The more this balance shifts—our old life for His new life—the more attractive our lives become to others.

> But now you must rid yourselves of all such things as these: anger, rage, malice, slander, and filthy language from your lips.
>
> Do not lie to each other, since you have taken off your old self with its practices and have put on the new self, which is being renewed in knowledge in the image of its Creator. ...
>
> Therefore, as God's chosen people, holy and dearly loved, clothe yourselves with compassion, kindness, humility, gentleness and patience. Bear with each other and forgive whatever grievances you may have against one another. Forgive as the Lord forgave you. And over all these virtues put on love, which binds them all together in perfect unity.
>
> —Colossians 3:8-14

Throughout the day, we can ask, *How would Jesus go about my work? How would He respond to my boss—or an obnoxious coworker?* When we demonstrate competence and character, our influence grows and our words take on authority.

Everyone Is a Preacher

John was a young doctor, establishing his practice in internal medicine, when his wife gave birth to their first child—a son with a serious birth defect. John's colleagues were well aware of the stress of learning to manage his workload while making the frequent 400-mile round trips to the children's hospital.

John may have had reason to be irritable, but he rarely was. One day during rounds, he discovered that a nurse had made a serious mistake that endangered a patient's life. He reprimanded the nurse firmly but respectfully, leaving her self-respect intact—a skill more doctors should learn. Unaware that a colleague overheard his reprimand, John felt a hand on his shoulder as he left the nursing station. His colleague said, "John, if you were a preacher, I'd go to your church."

The fact is, John is a preacher, as are we all. When people observe our competence, character, and genuine concern for others, we preach a powerful sermon.

TIMING MATTERS

God draws people into a relationship with Himself according to His timing, not ours. Solomon said: "There's a time to be silent and a time to speak" (Ecc. 3:7). It takes wisdom to know the difference.

When Jesus sent his disciples to preach the gospel, He said, "I am sending you out like sheep among wolves. Therefore be as shrewd as snakes and as innocent as doves" (Matt. 10:16). The Greek word *phronimos* translated shrewd means thoughtful or *discreet*. Jesus uses this word's positive connotation to remind us to think before we speak.

> **Peter's Advice**
> But in your hearts set apart Christ as Lord. Always be prepared to give an answer to everyone who asks you to give the reason for the hope that you have. But do this with gentleness and respect ...
> —1 Peter 3:15

Although we should always be ready and willing to speak up about our faith, note that Peter includes a condition: We are to be prepared to give an answer to *everyone who asks*. Ambushing people with the gospel when their hearts are not ready is not productive, nor is it gentle and respectful.

> "Jesus himself did not try to convert the two thieves on the cross; he waited until one of them turned to him."
> —Dietrich Bonhoeffer

So, how do we know when it is appropriate to speak? In addition to being sensitive to the Spirit's promptings, consider the following guidelines:

It is appropriate to talk about your faith ...

▶ **when opportunities arise out of growing friendships built around your work.** As you discuss work and life with your coworkers, informal mentions of spiritual truth will happen naturally, just as other topics of personal importance pop into your conversations.

▶ **when it naturally fits in the conversation.** Do not deliberately try to divert a discussion to a spiritual topic unrelated to the conversation. However, in the midst of a conversation about a business problem, for example, it could be appropriate to briefly mention how your faith guides your decisions.

▶ **when coworkers are comfortable with the discussion.** Keep your antennae up and change the subject if you sense discomfort.

▶ **when you are asked.** Questions open doors to address spiritual topics. You do not have to be a Bible expert to respond to such questions. Show your own personal interest in learning about that topic and simply and humbly explain what you have discovered at this point in your life. Encourage curiosity in order to create a safe environment for additional questions in the future.

▶ **when it does not take time away from what you or your coworker are paid to do.** Find time over a break, at lunch, or after work for longer discussions.

Cultivation Phase in a Nutshell

Possible Steps of Faith	CULTIVATION
Wary of Christians and truth claims	Speaks to the Heart
▼	**The Obstacles**
God and faith are irrelevant	Emotional Barriers: Denial, Indifference, Fear, Mistrust, Antagonism
▼	**Key Activities**
Aware that you are a Christian	Conversation Built on Competence and Character
▼	
Recognizes a difference in you	
▼	**The Goal**
Still has doubts about the Bible but likes you even though you are a Christian	Earning Trust and Creating Curiosity about Your Faith

If the idea of being a witness at work causes angst, take heart. In the next chapter, you will learn the third essential for spiritual influence—and how simple it can be.

The Bottom Line

Christ calls all believers to be His witnesses. But our lives always come before our lips.

Chapter 5

Keep It Simple

Nothing else is a substitute for the daily unspectacular witness
of the rank-and-file Christian.
—Ralph D. Winter

L ittle things do matter, and sometimes they matter most. This familiar adage defines the corporate culture at Southwest Airlines, where criteria for employment include "listening, caring, smiling, saying 'thank you,' and being warm." Valuing such seemingly small things continues to pay off in big ways. According to the Department of Transportation, Southwest consistently receives the fewest customer complaints of all major airlines.[1]

Bill's Experience

On my first visit to Southwest headquarters, I wanted to apply for a job on the spot. I saw firsthand how genuine care for people permeates the atmosphere of every corporate office and trickles down to employees at every level. Southwest co-founder Herb Kelleher believed that small actions and positive personal interactions between travelers and employees are key to success.

My friend Dave Ridley is Chief Marketing Officer and Senior Vice President of Business Development at Southwest. In a presentation, Dave told about a passenger who left her Bible in the seat pocket of a plane. When a flight attendant found it, she tracked down the passenger and mailed it (at her own expense) to the passenger.

Southwest's four million Facebook fans post stories like this regularly and say it is the little things keep them coming back.

In his book *Circle of Innovation*, business guru Tom Peters points out that the leaders at Ritz Carlton, one of the world's best and most successful hotel chains, believe in little things. Their mantra: "Little things = strategic advantage."

According to Peters, during one Ritz Carton stay, 25 to 30 employees "took a couple of seconds, stopped, looked me in the eye, and asked, 'How's everything going? Is there anything I can do for you?'"[2]

> Small things make a difference when it comes to spiritual influence in the workplace

Both Southwest and Ritz Carlton understand something important: Small things—showing concern through simple acts of kindness that often take only seconds—keep people coming back.

SMALL THINGS MAKE AN IMPACT

Small things also make a difference when it comes to spiritual influence in the workplace. Unfortunately, many Christians think spiritual influence is about "big things." This should not surprise us because Jesus' disciples made the same mistake. They were often fixated on big things.

James and John wanted to call down fire from heaven to put nonbelievers in their place.[3] Peter wanted to walk on water.[4] And knowing which disciples ranked highest and had the most authority was a big deal.[5] Throughout the Gospels, we see Jesus trying to teach His disciples that spiritual influence is not about doing big things. It is about being a servant.

> Jesus called them together and said, "You know that those who are regarded as rulers of the Gentiles lord it over them, and their high officials exercise authority over them. Not so with you. Instead, whoever wants to become great among you must be your servant, and whoever wants to be first must be slave of all. For even the Son of Man did not come to be served, but to serve, and to give his life as a ransom for many."
>
> —Mark 10:42-45

When it comes to carrying out His plans, it seems God has a penchant for small things that we may deem insignificant. Moses' wooden staff was nothing special, but God used it to confront the heart of the most powerful ruler of the ancient world. [6] David used a small stone to kill a giant.[7] With one word Jesus could have produced a catered meal for thousands, but instead He chose to use a small boy's lunch.[8]

God has not changed. He wants to use everyday things we may consider small—such as doing good work, reflecting Christ's character, and showing concern for others—to accomplish big things for His kingdom.

> Competence
> + Character
> + Concern
> = Spiritual Influence

Chapter four explained two components of becoming a person of spiritual influence:

1. **Competence:** doing our personal best work builds respect.

2. **Character:** reflecting Christ's character builds trust.

The third component of spiritual influence is showing concern for others.

3. **Concern:** performing small acts of kindness makes people want to listen.

Graciousness Stands Out in an Ungracious World

In a world grown accustomed to discourtesy and disrespect, where "me first, others second" is the norm, people who are others-centered stand out.

A 2013 survey asked, "Are Americans becoming ruder?" A whopping 77 percent answered yes.[9] Google *rudeness* and *narcissism* in the workplace, and you will come up with a list of characteristics that includes people who:

▶ belittle others

▶ do not share ideas with others

- ▶ take credit for things they did not do

- ▶ ask for help from coworkers, but do not return the favor

- ▶ spread gossip and backstab

- ▶ hoard resources

- ▶ kiss up to superiors

- ▶ do not stand up for others

- ▶ do what's best for themselves, not for the team

These traits are out of character for God's children.

> If you have any encouragement from being united with Christ, if any comfort from his love, if any fellowship with the Spirit, if any tenderness and compassion, then make my joy complete by being like-minded, having the same love, being one in spirit and purpose. Do nothing out of selfish ambition or vain conceit, but in humility consider others better than yourselves. Each of you should look not only to your own interests, but also to the interests of others.
>
> —Philippians 2:1–4

> Showing care and concern for others is not an option. It is what Christians do.

Showing care and concern for others is not an option. It is what Christians do—the natural outworking of our relationship with Christ.

Kind words and gracious actions come from within, not from obligation or religious duty. Our ability to consistently express grace and kindness toward others is directly related to understanding two things:

God's grace and kindness toward us is totally underserved. When this truth grasps our hearts, it compels us to extend grace and kindness to others.

> Therefore, as God's chosen people, holy and dearly loved, clothe yourselves with compassion, kindness, humility, gentleness and patience. Bear with each other and forgive whatever grievances you may have against one another. Forgive as the Lord forgave you.
>
> —Colossians 3:12-13

Christ is alive in us, and He gives us the power to love others.

> For I can do everything through Christ, who gives me strength.
>
> —Philippians 4:13 (NLT)

WHAT GRACE LOOKS LIKE

When we show concern toward others through our words and actions, people have the opportunity to see Jesus in us. This can soften the hardest of hearts.

In Our Words

What we say and how we say it speaks volumes about who we are, what motivates us, and how much we care about others.

The apostle Paul allows little wiggle room when it comes to thoughtless words: "Do not let any unwholesome talk come out of your mouths, but only what is helpful for building others up according to their needs, that it may benefit those who listen" (Eph. 4:29). Even when we must deliver a negative message, we are to "speak the truth in love" (Eph. 4:15).

> Consider this wisdom about words from the book of Proverbs:
> - A gentle answer turns away wrath, but a harsh word stirs up anger (Prov. 15:1).
> - Through patience a ruler can be persuaded, and a gentle tongue can break a bone (Prov. 25:15).
> - The lips of the righteous know what is fitting, but the mouth of the wicked only what is perverse (Prov. 10:32).
> - An honest answer is like a kiss on the lips (Prov. 24:26).
> - A word aptly spoken is like apples of gold in settings of silver (Prov. 25:11).

Here are a dozen simple ways our words can show grace and kindness. Note any ideas that fit for your personality, position, and workplace environment.

► Go out of your way to put in a good word for someone to the appropriate person.

► Express interest when someone shows you family photos.

► Make it a point to look people in the eyes and say "good morning" when you arrive and "hello" when you pass in the hallway.

► Say "thank you" to someone who faithfully performs a behind-the-scenes job.

► Celebrate with someone over a success.

► Honor someone by asking for their advice.

► Remind someone how much their work matters.

► Remember the name of a coworker's spouse.

► Remember a coworker's birthday or anniversary.

► Go out of your way to let coworkers know you appreciate something they did or said.

► Point out someone's giftedness and how it blesses others on the team.

► Take the blame for a problem without blaming others.

In How We Listen

Our willingness to listen and receive input from others sends a powerful message: *I care what you think; you have something valuable to contribute.* When we ask questions and listen with focused attention and a humble spirit, we invite trust and cooperation in business and personal relationships.

> My dear brothers, take note of this: Everyone should be quick to listen, slow to speak and slow to become angry.
>
> —James 1:19

Consider these suggestions for gracious listening:

▶ Face the person who is speaking to you and maintain eye contact. Don't look out the window or scan the room. Put aside papers, cell phone, and other distractions.

▶ Listen without judging or mentally criticizing the speaker. And do not jump to conclusions. Let the speaker finish, and ask for clarification about things you question before you respond.

▶ When listening to someone talk about a problem, do not interrupt with advice or solutions. Many times, people need a sounding board, not an answer. Wait a while, then get the speaker's permission to share your idea or solution.

▶ Show empathy through your facial expressions. This demonstrates genuine concern for what the speaker is saying.

▶ Greet someone in the hall by saying, "How are you?" Stop and sincerely listen to the response.

▶ Ask meaningful questions about things that are important to others and actively listen to what they say.

▶ Listen for the aspirations and fears of others. Pray that God will show you appropriate ways to encourage them.

▶ Actively seek to understand rather than win an argument. You could easily win the fight but lose the war.

▶ Focus on understanding the speaker, not on calculating your rebuttal.

▶ Create safe space for people to disagree with you by listening to criticism without blowing up.

The way we respond to daily stress and success reveals whether we care more about others or ourselves.

77

In Our Actions

Gracious words and listening should be accompanied by corresponding actions. Use the following ideas to spur your thinking about how to show your concern for others:

► Help someone clean up a spill.

► Finish a task for someone who is tired.

► Write a coworker a handwritten note of encouragement or congratulations.

► Offer to hold a seat for a coworker who will be joining a meeting after it starts.

> Pray daily that God will show you ways to be a blessing to others.

► If you have the authority, allow a person to stay home or leave early when a family member is ill.

► Offer to run an errand for someone who is under a tight deadline.

► Go the extra mile. Fill the printer paper tray. Leave the conference room cleaner than you found it.

► Always clean up after yourself in the employee kitchen. And if you know a coworker is time-strapped or late for a meeting, offer to clean up for him or her.

► Be patient with someone who is having a hard time catching on to something.

► Offer to work on a religious holiday for someone of a different faith.

► When you meet a coworker for a crack-of-dawn work session, bring muffins and coffee.

► Fill an emergency basket for the office with a small sewing kit, Band-Aids, pain reliever, antacids and such. Invite coworkers to help themselves.

▶ Bring dinner in a cooler to the office for a single parent.

▶ Give someone your place in line.

▶ Offer to help anyone who needs assistance opening a door, reaching for an elevator button, or carrying packages.

▶ Bring treats to a meeting when no one is expecting it.

▶ Offer to let someone borrow something for a special occasion.

▶ Donate to a coworker who is raising money for a cause.

▶ Invite a single coworker to your home for a holiday meal.

▶ Make notes about your coworkers' interests so you can talk to them about things they enjoy.

▶ Help a coworker fix a flat tire in the parking lot.

▶ Share your knowledge with someone who needs help.

> The main test of our dealings with the world is whether the men and women we associate with are better or worse for it.
>
> —George MacDonald

Start a Movement

Whether we work on a factory floor, in a cramped cubical, or in the corner office, each of us is significant and every gift is important in God's master plan to draw people to Him. He has given us the privilege of being part of the world's redemption. Never forget small things—a word of encouragement or a simple act of kindness—can be used by God to accomplish big things.

> **Kindness Is Contagious**
> A study by the National Academy of Sciences concluded that a single act of kindness can spread between individuals and across time, from Person A to Person B, from Person B to Person C, and from Person C to Person D.[10]

Envision what could happen if Christians in workplaces around the world focused on spreading God's grace through simple acts of kindness. We could transform the atmosphere of our workplaces and build spiritual influence that God could use to draw millions to Him.

Bill's Experience

My son James entered the job market in 2008 just as the bottom dropped out of the economy. After months of searching for a position where he could use his gifts and education, he took a job as a sales associate at a large retail chain. The position was less than ideal, but James did his work diligently and brought his positive, helpful attitude to work every day.

Although many employees made little or no effort to be helpful or friendly, James worked at building relationships with his coworkers.

After a few months, he received his first promotion. His team won numerous sales awards, and he rose to assistant manager of the company's flagship store. James also earned the trust of many coworkers, which opened doors for conversations about faith over lunch and during breaks.

His ideal job finally came along, but he still goes back to the store to stay in touch. Sometimes he brings in pizza when everyone is working long hours during big sales events.

It doesn't take a lot of light to light up a dark room or a dark workplace. "In the same way, let your light shine before men, that they may see your good deeds and praise your Father in heaven" (Matt. 5:16).

The Bottom Line

In God's plan to take the gospel to the human race, small things add up to big things that make a big difference.

Chapter 6

Fostering Curiosity

Storytelling is the most powerful way to put ideas into the world today.
—Robert McKee

From Genesis to Revelation, the Bible is packed with stories of birth, death, love, hate, murder, deceit, courage, sacrifice, revenge, treason, war, and every other kind of drama imaginable. God could have provided an indexed guidebook for living life on earth. Instead, He gave us the Bible, His inspired Word, and filled it with stories, all "useful for teaching, rebuking, correcting and training in righteousness" (2 Tim. 3:16).

Stories shape information into meaning and help others visualize who we are and what we believe.

"A story is the only way to activate parts in the brain so that a listener turns the story into their own idea and experience," according to Dr. Uri Hasson of Princeton.

When we tell stories to others that have helped us shape our thinking and way of life, our story can have the same effect on them too. When we hear a good story, we develop empathy with the teller because we experience the events for ourselves.[1]

In evangelism, a story is a potent yet understated way to communicate truth without confrontation. Telling a story about a personal experience with God or about how a principle in the Bible changed our lives, or family, or career, can resonate with an unbeliever's longings and allow us to connect on an emotional level.

> Faith Flags are a nonthreatening way to gently introduce faith into a conversation.

A story portrays truth in a tangible and authentic way. It opens a window for unbelievers to get a glimpse of what it is like to be a person of faith and can give them a reason to rethink negative notions they may hold about Christians or Christianity. Also, people remember stories. When the conversation is over, they have the opportunity to ponder stories at their own pace.

Faith Flags and Faith Stories are nonthreatening tools that harness the amazing power of storytelling. They help create curiosity about faith and open doors for further discussion.

FAITH FLAGS

A Faith Flag is a brief mention or statement about God, the Bible, or prayer in the natural course of conversation that communicates we have a spiritual dimension. A Faith Flag ...

- ▶ provides a snapshot of who we are and what we believe.

- ▶ helps identify us as individuals to whom faith is important.

- ▶ can open up opportunities for further discussion about spiritual topics.

Examples of Faith Flags

What a Faith Flag might sound like:

- ▶ When someone untangles a knotty dilemma:
  "I'm really glad you're on the team. God sure gave you a keen mind for solving problems."

▶ When someone expresses a concern about a child:
"I'll cover for you anytime you need to leave work and take your son to the doctor. I'll also pray for your son."

▶ When someone compliments your presentation:
"Thanks for your encouragement. If you only knew how petrified I was this time yesterday. God calmed me down and helped me to focus."

▶ When presenting at a sales meeting:
"I'm happy to report that we hit our goal! Although the quarter had a slow start, everyone worked really hard and God blessed our efforts."

▶ In a conversation about parenting:
"My wife and I were thrilled to get a positive report from our son's teacher. We've been reading from the book of Proverbs at breakfast about living wisely. At least one person in our family is making progress!"

GUIDELINES FOR RAISING FAITH FLAGS

For Faith Flags to be productive, we should keep the following guidelines in mind:

1. Make it fit.

A Faith Flag should occur as a natural part of a conversation. Although intentional, it is not contrived—nor is it a random statement interjected into the conversation. It is a simple expression of the reality of faith as it relates to a given conversation.

2. Keep it short.

A Faith Flag should take no longer than a few seconds. Typically only a sentence or two, a Faith Flag is a comment, not a lengthy commentary.

> Faith Flags only take a few seconds.

3. Keep it general.

We should not name a particular church, denomination, pastor, or spiritual leader. If listeners hold negative feelings toward a particular group or person, they may transfer those feelings to us, closing the door to further discussion. The goal is to identify ourselves as individuals who value faith, prayer, the Bible, and God.

4. Keep it positive.

We must not use faith as an excuse for avoiding certain behaviors. For example, in a discussion about a company party, we should avoid polarizing statements such as, "I used to drink before I became a Christian." Although such a remark may be true, it defines our faith by what we are against rather than what we are for.

5. Watch for a response.

We should look for, but not expect, a response to a Faith Flag. A verbal reply can help gauge if and where the Holy Spirit is at work in the person's life. Body language is also a clue to someone's interest or comfort level in talking about spiritual topics.

6. Respect a negative or silent response.

A negative response indicates the need for more cultivation. If a listener offers no response, we must not push. Instead, we should give others the time and freedom for processing new information about us.

Bill's Experience

As the plane took off, I engaged in polite conversation with a woman sitting in the window seat and learned that she was an artist. She grew quiet and went back to her book when she learned that I was a theologian. I closed my eyes and tried to rest.

When the plane broke through the cloud cover and reached cruising altitude, the prompting of the Holy Spirit interrupted my nap. I opened my eyes and noticed that my seatmate was staring at the breathtaking sunset.

> "Beautiful isn't it?" I commented casually. "It's amazing how God paints us a new work of art every evening, and no two are alike."
>
> Her response to my Faith Flag surprised me. For the next hour, she told me more about her life. We talked about what the Bible says about God's ability to meet her needs in the difficult circumstances she was facing.

God can use a Faith Flag to pique a person's interest and to cultivate a desire to know more.

FAITH STORIES

A Faith Story is another powerful way to communicate spiritual truth in an inviting form. It briefly describes a particular

> Rather than using facts to beat on the mind's front door, which is often bolted from within, a story allows truth to enter through the backdoor of the heart.

instance when we had an encounter with God or a time when we learned an important spiritual lesson. It lets the listener see how God is at work, making a meaningful and practical difference in our lives.

A Faith Story ...

► is a glimpse of what it is like to be a child of God and what active real-life faith looks like.

► corresponds to a need or circumstance in the listener's life and may stimulate questions or comments.

► helps explain why there is something different about us.

> **Walt's Experience**
>
> As a physician, I see many people who are facing difficult medical problems. The following Faith Story has opened many doors for me to speak to patients about how God can work in the toughest situation in their lives.
>
> When my daughter Kate was eleven, she experienced a life-threatening grand mal seizure. We rushed her to the hospital, where it took our family doctor over an hour to stop the seizure.
>
> By that time, Kate had stopped breathing and was put on a ventilator. In the ICU, doctors told us that her brain wave was flat, and they weren't sure if medicines or brain death had caused it.

> Barb and I stayed by Kate's bedside. We hugged, and we cried. We were in total shock. Later that evening, a friend came to the hospital. He didn't have a lot of advice or fancy words. He just showed us how to pray.
>
> We spent that night in prayer by Kate's bedside and began a practice that God has used in our lives ever since.

Examples of Faith Stories

The following examples of Faith Stories can help each of us think of our own experiences and how these personal encounters with God can communicate life-changing truths to others.

▶ When someone mentions a financial issue:
Financial problems are tough. When I was in grad school and my wife gave birth to our first child, we were beyond broke. Our hospital bills were more than we expected, and I didn't know how we'd pay for my tuition or the rent—and both were due. I was desperate, and all I knew to do was pray. The next week, we received a check for the exact amount we needed from someone who wanted to remain anonymous. I have no doubt God used that person to answer my prayer.

▶ When someone shares about a life-threatening experience:
I can relate to how your wreck must have scared you. A few years ago, I had a bad wreck on a two-lane highway. I'd been pushing hard, working way too much, and I fell asleep at the wheel. I crossed into the other lane and hit a trailer pulled behind a truck. People who saw my car couldn't believe I lived through it. I know I'm alive because God has a purpose for my life.

▶ In response to a comment about how you handled a difficult situation at work:
Thank you, I haven't always been able to respond this way. I had high anxiety down to a science until a couple of years ago. My mentor at the time noticed how stress was affecting my work and my personality. We met once a week over the next few months

*to study what the Bible says about experiencing peace. My life
hasn't been the same since.*

▶ In a conversation about a lost business opportunity:
*A few years ago, I had a business deal fail, and it about killed
me. I'd worked on it for months and put everything else on hold.
The bank was calling, I couldn't sleep at night, and I was having
chest pains. I had no other option but to trust God with my
business. I realized I needed to work smart and do my best work,
but in the end, God controls the results. I don't like to lose, but I
have peace of mind knowing God is running the show.*

Guidelines for Telling Faith Stories

For a Faith Story to be productive, we should
keep the following guidelines in mind.

> Faith Stories should take no more than two minutes.

1. **Make it fit.**
   Like Faith Flags, Faith Stories should fit the natural flow of a
   conversation. They relate to topics being discussed.

2. **Keep it brief**.
   Faith Stories should take no more than two minutes. We should
   avoid the temptation of unloading a spiritual dump truck if we
   detect spiritual interest. People need time and space to process
   what we say.

> Even when someone asks questions, keep the conversation short. This
> helps avoid the danger of running too far ahead and losing the listener's
> attention. Let curiosity pave the way for future conversation. There are
> people God is drawing, so my prayer is that God would bring me together
> with them in his timing. I am also proactive in this by saying something
> spiritual in the conversation that the other person can pick up on. If they
> pick up on it, I'll go as far as they are willing to talk. If you say something
> and they don't respond, that time is probably not the best to go on with it.
> Early on, I offended people by going on when they didn't want to hear it.
> —Norm Miller, Chairman, Interstate Batteries

3. Trust the Holy Spirit.

We should resist attempts to convict listeners after we tell Faith Stories. Our role is to allow our words to settle into the hearts of others—and let the Holy Spirit do His work.

> Our role is to allow our words to settle into the hearts of others—and let the Holy Spirit do His work.

We cannot take a step toward God for someone else. A relationship with God is a personal journey, not a group decision. If we allow our self-worth to get wrapped up in the responses of others, our behavior is likely to become manipulative. Although God can use us, He is the One who convicts people of the truth and draws people to Himself.

4. Be authentic and wise.

People appreciate authenticity, not perfection. It is okay to reveal our struggles to nonbelievers. Faith in Jesus does not solve all of life's problems or make anyone perfect. We should, however, avoid parts of our stories that could be embarrassing or awkward for others.

> If the world can write us off as super-spiritual people who don't have needs and problems like theirs, they'll write off God as irrelevant. But once they see and know that we are all alike and that we have common needs and problems and interests, they'll be far more curious when we say, "God makes a difference."
>
> —Rebecca Pippert

5. Be humble.

When sharing a Faith Story, we must take special care not to communicate in a way that sounds condescending or benevolently superior. The only reason we know and believe the truth is because God chose to awaken our hearts, open our ears, and reveal Himself to us. This truth should make us the most humble people on earth.

6. Stay even-tempered.

We should not be surprised if we receive a negative or offensive response when we tell a Faith Story. We are in a battle, and Satan has blinded the minds of unbelievers.

> The god of this age has blinded the minds of unbelievers, so that they cannot see the light of the gospel of the glory of Christ, who is the image of God.
>
> —2 Corinthians 4:4

It is acceptable to correct misunderstandings about our Faith Stories or to clarify what God has done in our lives, but we should not turn faith conversations into debates. Our goal is to win the hearts of our friends, not to win arguments.

WATCH THE LANGUAGE

Jargon frustrates outsiders who want to understand. Professional groups and large organizations often use insider language indecipherable to the uninitiated. Christians are guilty as well. We regularly use words like *salvation*, *fellowship*, and *the gospel* in conversations with fellow Christians. It is easy to forget that words such these can leave our coworkers and friends confused and even repelled.

> When speaking with nonbelievers, we should avoid terms that could be confusing, misunderstood, or perceived negatively.

As recently as the last century, Americans were more theologically literate. In today's culture, we cannot assume others understand biblical terms that are rich with meaning for our faith.

For example, the word *lost* describes our separation from God and inability to find our way back. However, most nonbelievers do not appreciate being labeled as *lost*. And the term *born again* has come to describe a narrow-minded, conservative, politically right-wing person.

Sin is another term that causes misunderstanding. Sin is often viewed by unbelievers as *thou-shalt-not* behavior on a list of arbitrary Christian rules. Since most people are averse to arbitrary rules, using the term *sin* to explain the problem between God and humans, may not produce conviction. It is not likely to generate the desire for forgiveness they should feel for violating God's standards.

When speaking with non-Christians, we should avoid terms that could be confusing, misunderstood, or perceived negatively. Although the following alternatives do not capture the richness of biblical terms, they may help unchurched colleagues better understand what we say.

Terms:	Alternatives to consider:
Lost	Separated from God
Salvation	Knowing God personally
Faith	Believe in, trust in, rely upon
Repent	Change mind/heart
Justified	Just as if I never did wrong; declared "not guilty"
Redeemed	The penalty was paid for my wrongdoing
Saved	Reconnected with God
Sanctified	To become all God created us to be

If history were taught in the form of stories, it would never be forgotten.
—Rudyard Kipling

Create Your Own Faith Stories

Use these suggestions to develop your own faith stories:

Step 1: Make a list of times when you had a significant personal encounter with God. It may have been an instance when…

► God did something meaningful or significant in your life.

► you knew God was at work.

► an experience taught you that God loves you.

▶ God broke through to you and taught you something important you will never forget.

▶ God worked through you to accomplish His purposes.

Step 2: Choose one or two of these experiences and write a brief Faith Story about each.

We should take care that our stories are formed around biblical truth and remind ourselves that they are holy because they are part of God's greater story. He can use our stories to guide people to a relationship with Jesus today—and continue to use them in years and generations to come.

The Bottom Line

Stories can resonate with the listener's longings and evoke consideration of gospel truth on an emotional level.

Chapter 7

Building a Spiritual Network

We should not only use all the brains we have,
but all that we can borrow.
—Woodrow Wilson

Busyness is the new normal in America. In the not-too-distant past, "Good" or "Very well, thank you" were common responses when someone asked, "How are you?" Responses to the same question today range from *"Really* busy" to "Utterly exhausted."

> "Somewhere around the end of the 20th century, busyness became not just a way of life but a badge of honor. And life, sociologists say, became an exhausting everydayathon. People now tell pollsters that they're too busy to register to vote, too busy to date, to make friends outside the office, to take a vacation, to sleep, to have sex."[1]

So, how does busyness affect evangelism? Well, one thing we know for sure: God is not scratching His head, saying, *Wow, I didn't think about how busy schedules in the twenty-first century would affect My plan for taking the gospel to the world.*

God's evangelism strategy for twenty-first-century Christians who can travel ten miles in ten minutes to a job site is the same strategy that worked for first-century Christians who traveled three hours—on a good day with a lively donkey—to cover similar ground: teamwork.

GOD INVENTED TEAMWORK

> Teamwork:
> The fuel that produces uncommon results in common people.
> —Andrew Carnegie

Some think of teamwork as a modern management strategy, but it has always been God's universal rule for getting things done. God Himself, the Trinity, is a team of three (Father, Son, and Holy Spirit), working together—each playing a different role—to create, sustain, and redeem creation.[2]

God has used teams to accomplish His work throughout history. A few examples:

▶ He created humankind as a male/female team to do His work.[3]

▶ He chose a team of artisans to build the Tabernacle.[4]

▶ Nehemiah used a team to rebuild Jerusalem's wall.[5]

▶ Solomon explained the wisdom of working as a team.

> Two are better than one, because they have a good return for their work: If one falls down, his friend can help him up.
> —Ecclesiastes 4:9-10

▶ Jesus called a team of twelve to work closely with Him.[6]

▶ Jesus sent out seventy disciples in teams of two to proclaim the coming of the kingdom.[7]

▶ Throughout the book of Acts, we see the early church working in teams.[8]

▶ The Greek word *allēlōn*, which means "one another, reciprocally, mutually," emphasizing teamwork, is used one hundred times in the New Testament.

IT TAKES A NETWORK

Physicians know the importance of using a "consult network" of physicians in

> God never intended evangelism to be a solo endeavor.

different specialties, whom they know and trust, for the purposes of referring patients and drawing on each other's expertise.

In the business world, networking is a time-honored tradition. Like-minded businesspeople network to build relationships, share information, and generate mutually beneficial opportunities.

When it comes to evangelism, we can learn from both the healthcare and business networking models to create a team of like-minded Christians who work together for Kingdom purposes.

Walt's Experience

Managing time is a constant challenge for physicians. When John Hartman and I were partners in family medicine, we faced a dilemma. Sometimes we would raise Faith Flags and patients would want to talk further. Stopping to have lengthy conversations put us way behind schedule, which was not fair to our other patients or staff.

To solve the problem, John and I implemented a strategy that one of my professors, noted hand surgeon Dr. Paul Brand, had recommended. We created a spiritual consult network for referring patients with spiritual needs we could not handle at the time. This made perfect sense because we had already created a consult network of medical professionals we could use to refer patients whose physical or emotional needs were beyond our training.

Dr. Brand put it this way, "We need to know and have available to us (on call, as it were) other people who can participate with us in this great work of witnessing to the love of God. I believe we should know people in our church and in our hospital ... so that in our busyness, when we cannot give as much time as we ought to give, we can call someone else to help. It would be wise to have a list of other members of the body of Christ who could help us in this great work." [9]

BENEFITS OF A SPIRITUAL NETWORK

God never intended evangelism to be a solo endeavor. Working with a formal or informal network of like-minded Christians committed to fulfilling their roles in the Great Commission is both biblical and practical. Creating a Spiritual Network can help our efforts to spread the gospel in at least five ways.

> I can do what you can't do, and you can do what I can't do; together we can do great things.
> —Mother Teresa

1. A Spiritual Network can help overcome our limitations.

None of us has what it takes to do everything we need to do, much less what we want to do. We are limited by ...

▶ **Time:** Twenty-four hours a day is all we have.

▶ **Space:** Each of us can only be one place at a given time.

▶ **Ability:** None of us has all the gifts.

If we choose to work solo, it is highly likely we will take on commitments God never intended us to tackle alone, overvalue our abilities, and usurp work God gifted others to do.

> Do not think of yourself more highly than you ought, but rather think of yourself with sober judgment, in accordance with the measure of faith God has given you. Just as each of us has one body with many members, and these members do not all have the same function, so in Christ we who are many form one body, and each member belongs to all the others. We have different gifts, according to the grace given us.
> —Romans 12:3-6

Just as a relay team passes the baton from one member to another and works toward a common goal, a Spiritual Network brings together the help we need to accomplish more than any of us can do alone.

2. A Spiritual Network allows the body of Christ to work as God intended.

In the first century, networks of Christians with diverse gifts and occupations worked together to propel the gospel message far and wide.[10] By divine design, no one person has all the gifts needed to fulfill the Great Commission. We need other members of the body of Christ to join our efforts.

Typically, an individual's journey to faith is not one big leap, but many small steps. Nor is it due to the influence of only one person. In a relay, one person crosses the finish line, but it would not have happened without each person on the team fulfilling his or her role. The same is true in evangelism.

Most people can name a number of individuals whom God used to influence their spiritual journey. Think about your own journey and the various people who helped you take a step closer to Christ.

Bill's Experience

I counted thirteen people who helped me to take small steps toward faith: my parents, a high school Sunday school teacher, a girlfriend, the girlfriend's pastor, two upperclassmen who served as advisors to freshmen in my dorm at Southern Methodist University, a seminary student who hung out on our floor, a friend who drug me to a Bible study, and four speakers at different gospel-focused events sponsored by Campus Crusade for Christ (CRU). I trusted Christ at one of those events.

Walt's Experience

CRU staff member Rich McGee led me to Christ when I was a student at Louisiana State University (LSU). In addition to Rich, God used twenty-eight people to cultivate the soil of my heart and scatter seeds of truth: my parents, my Aunt Martha, my grandmother, two Episcopal priests, friends in a small group at a church camp, a high school girlfriend, a friend and high school football teammate, a campus pastor at LSU and members of his church, a speaker who presented the gospel at an event, three LSU football players, a CRU staff member who hung around my dorm, and an ancestor who wrote that he prayed for the salvation of family members in generations to come.

3. A Spiritual Network helps prevent burnout.

To earn the trust of our coworkers is an honor and a privilege. It can also be a hazard because every person in our workplace has needs—even those whose lives may outwardly appear near-perfect. They have relational issues, financial problems, health concerns, work struggles, fears about the future, and personal insecurities.

> No one can whistle a symphony.
> It takes an orchestra to play it.
> —Halford E. Luccock

Remember: a need does not necessitate a call. Since we have a limited amount of time and energy, when we say *yes* to one thing, we are saying *no* to something else. Satan loves to see Christians say *yes* to too many things—even good things. He knows over commitment will render us ineffective and steal our joy.

Working without a team puts us on a fast track to exhaustion and burnout. It is also an indication that we need to assess our motives for taking on more than God intended us to handle.

When Moses let his sense of responsibility run away with him in the desert, Jethro asked why he was trying to solve every person's problem, Moses answered, "Because the people come to me."

So Jethro gave him some advice.

What you are doing is not good. You and these people who come to you will only wear yourselves out. The work is too heavy for you; you cannot handle it alone." (Ex. 18:17-18)

A Spiritual Network prevents us from making this mistake. Like Moses, we need to find others we can rely on to meet needs we are not called to handle.

4. A Spiritual Network helps keep priorities in line.

God is sovereign. He brings into our lives nonbelievers whom we would love to see come to faith. He also places us under authority at work. If we chronically neglect our work or other God-given commitments to meet too many spiritual needs, something is motivating us besides God. We not only disobey Him,[11] we paint a distorted picture of what it means to follow Christ at work. When meeting a spiritual need tempts us to neglect important commitments, it is time to ask someone in our Spiritual Network to step in.

5. A Spiritual Network provides much-needed encouragement.

God is the consummate encourager. He knows life in a fallen world is difficult, and that physical and emotional fatigue can cause us to lose hope. He imparts words of encouragement Himself and calls us to encourage each other as well.

> And let us consider how we may spur one another on toward love and good deeds. Let us not give up meeting together, as some are in the habit of doing, but let us encourage one another—and all the more as you see the Day approaching.
> —Hebrews 10:24-25

If ever there existed a strong personality who could go it alone, it was Paul. But note that he not only worked with a team, he drew encouragement from team members, especially Barnabas, the Son of Encouragement.[12] Paul wrote about the value of encouragement in almost all his letters. For example:

- ▶ **To the Romans:** I long to see you so that I may impart to you some spiritual gift to make you strong—that is, that you and I may be mutually encouraged by each other's faith (1:11-12).

- ▶ **To the Philippians:** Because of my chains, most of the brothers in the Lord have been encouraged to speak the word of God more courageously and fearlessly (1:14).

- ▶ **To the Colossians:** These are the only Jews among my fellow workers for the kingdom of God, and they have proved a comfort to me (4:11).

- **To the Thessalonians:** Therefore encourage one another and build each other up, just as in fact you are doing (1 Thess. 5:11).

- **To Philemon:** Your love has given me great joy and encouragement, because you, brother, have refreshed the hearts of the saints (1:7).

Encouragement is a powerful benefit of a spiritual network.

BUILDING A SPIRITUAL NETWORK

Developing a Spiritual Network does not have to be complicated, but it does take thought and time.

1. Begin with prayer.

Asking God for wisdom about choosing team members is vital. He delights in revealing His will to those who ask.

> Then he said to his disciples, "The harvest is plentiful but the workers are few. Ask the Lord of the harvest, therefore, to send out workers into his harvest field."
>
> —Matthew 9:37-38

2. Consider depth of character.

When choosing team members, these qualities rank high.

- Trustworthy
- Has some degree of spiritual maturity
- Exhibits competence, character, and concern at work
- Knows how to lovingly convey spiritual truth
- Servant-minded
- Humble
- Available
- Maintains confidentiality
- May have expertise in an area, such as counseling or apologetics

3. Think broad.

When casting a net for a Spiritual Network, it is more productive to use a broad perspective rather than a narrow focus.

Known Connections. Creating a written list of all known believers is an excellent launching point for a Spiritual Network.

Other Coworkers. Raising Faith Flags in the workplace will often surface other Christians.

B2B. Christians who work in other companies are great connections.

> **Bill's Experience**
> My friend Audie, who owns a manufacturing company, is a committed Christian. One of his customers in another state is also a believer. Whenever Audie makes a sales call, the customer schedules lunch with a nonbeliever he thinks would benefit from meeting Audie. Sometimes, the conversation moves to a spiritual topic, but even when it does not, Audie and his customer always pray together and encourage each other spiritually.

Customers and clients. When a client is a Christian, scheduling personal time to gauge interest in working informally on kingdom ventures can prove mutually beneficial.

People in the same profession or industry sector. Christian brothers and sisters who understand the unique challenges of a particular field can be important team members.

4. Think creatively.

Beyond the workplace, there are others vital to a strong Spiritual Network.

Pastors and counselors. Someone may need spiritual or emotional help beyond the expertise of a layperson. Pastors and counselors also have connections to individuals or groups with specific expertise.

Take your pastor to lunch and challenge him or her to join your Spiritual Network.

One Pastor's Commitment

After attending "The Saline Solution" conference, a pastor assembled a team of Christian physicians interested in making a spiritual impact in their practices. Here's what this pastor committed to do for them:

► He met with them to pray for opportunities to raise Faith Flags.
► He asked about opportunities they had to share their faith.
► He regularly visited them in their workplaces.
► He connected them with potential employees.
► He provided counsel upon request.

Marketplace chaplains. Hundreds of thousands of employees are served by company chaplains who work both independently and through two national chaplaincy providers.[13]

Local and national workplace ministries. More than a thousand ministries serve people in the workplace. These organizations connect Christians in the workplace and offer significant resources online, in print, and through personal interaction.

Visit *www.CenterForFaithAndWork.com/ministries* for a growing list of national and local workplace ministries.

Get Started

A Spiritual Network created today can make an impact for God's kingdom tomorrow. Remember this: God does not need an army to accomplish His work. One person can make a difference—but not alone. Our efforts are multiplied when we work with others, even with just one other person.

If two of you on earth agree about anything you ask for, it will be done for you by my Father in heaven. For where two or three come together in my name, there am I with them.

—Matthew 18:19–20

The Bottom Line

Evangelism is a team activity. Network with others for maximum spiritual impact.

Chapter 8

No Impact Without Contact

Community is no longer "natural" under the conditions of late modernity, and so it will require an intentionality that is unfamiliar and perhaps uncomfortable to most Christians and most churches.
—*James Davison Hunter*

The term *cocooning* was coined by trend forecaster Faith Popcorn to describe Americans who were socializing less and hunkering down at home to protect themselves from the harsh realities of the outside world. This trend fed a burgeoning do-it-yourself industry and sparked home-entertainment innovations, such as video game systems, rec rooms, and media rooms.

Today, thanks to technology, cocooning has morphed into super-cocooning.[1] Isolation has never been easier. After all, why go to the hassle of planning dinner and a movie with friends when we can have dinner delivered to our door and watch a favorite film from the comfort of our couch?

> Never be afraid to trust an unknown future to a known God.
>
> —Corrie ten Boom

Fear is also accelerating the trend toward isolation. With disturbing regularity, we learn of shootings at schools, theaters, malls, and military posts. These events, along other random acts of terrorism, heighten our sense of unrest.

"Everybody is nervous, really nervous," says Popcorn. "I think we're looking for protection. Almost like the Jetsons, we want to walk around in a little bubble."[2]

Impact on the Workplace

Cocooning makes us less social, which affects Hollywood, professional sports, tourism, and the restaurant industry.[3] It also affects the office environment, as more people work from home and connect digitally. Even those at the office are prone to cocoon in their cubicles and text coworkers twenty feet away.

> ... the last several decades have witnessed a striking diminution of regular contacts with our friends and neighbors. We spend less time in conversation over meals; we exchange visits less often; we engage less often in leisure activities that encourage casual social action; we spend more time watching (admittedly some of it in the presence of others) and less time doing. We know our neighbors less well, and we see old friends less often.[4]
>
> —Robert D. Putnam
> *Bowling Alone*

Cocooning also affects evangelism. Many Christians try to insulate themselves from the world in a Christian bubble. They cluster with Christians at work, after work, and on the weekends, sheltering themselves from the world and avoiding nonbelievers.

> Living life in a Christian ghetto might prevent the message of Christ from being diluted, but it also prevents it from being delivered ... Isolation is a bizarre attempt to cure the disease of sin by quarantining the doctors.
>
> —Lem Howard

Problem is, it is hard to play our roles in the Great Commission, helping nonbelievers take steps toward Jesus, if we avoid contact with them. And when we isolate, we are allowing the world—the world we want to avoid—to shape our lifestyle. Paul challenged Christians in Rome about this.

> Do not conform any longer to the pattern of this world, but be transformed by the renewing of your mind. Then you will be able to test and approve what God's will is—his good, pleasing and perfect will. (Rom. 12:2)

SALTY CHRISTIANS

In the Sermon on the Mount, Jesus told His followers, "You are the salt of the earth."[5] His comments have spurred varied interpretations ever since.

Salt was critical to first-century civilization as a food preservative, as well as a flavoring.[6] Salt was also used for medicinal and antiseptic purposes.[7] It was a vital part of Hebrew worship too.

Today, we know that salt is essential to life itself. Every function of the body is dependent on sodium levels. Breathing, circulation, thinking, digestion, movement, growth—our entire physical existence—depends on the correct saline level in our bodies. Too much or too little is a matter of life or death. Literally.

However we interpret Jesus' words, one thing is clear: For salt to do its work, it has to make contact, so isolation is not an option for followers of Jesus.

For more than 30 years, Jesus lived in the misery and depravity of our fallen world so that we could have a relationship with Him.[8] He spent time with the kind

> For salt to do its work, it has to make contact, so isolation is not an option for followers of Jesus.

of people the religious leaders avoided—so much time, in fact, he was called a friend of sinners.[9] Jesus calls us to do the same. We have been sent into the world, not to live in a spiritual cocoon.

In His prayer for His disciples, Jesus asked the Father not to isolate us from the world, but to insulate us from Satan's corrupting influence.[10]

> My prayer is not that you take them out of the world but that you protect them from the evil one. They are not of the world, even as I am not of it. Sanctify them by the truth; your word is truth. As you sent me into the world, I have sent them into the world.
>
> —John 17:15–18

> **The workplace is the one place where Christians and nonbelievers are forced to spend significant time together.**

Contrary to Jesus intent, many Christians lose significant connection with nonbelieving friends within a few years of conversion. This is why the workplace is so strategic to the spread of the gospel. It is the one place where Christians are forced to rub shoulders with nonbelievers and have the opportunity to develop deeper relationships.

FINDING COMMON GROUND

It is no accident that we regularly work with certain people. God places these people in our lives. They are our mission field. As we engage in the cultivation process with them—demonstrating competence, character, and concern—and take opportunities to raise Faith Flags and tell Faith Stories, some of them may run the other way. Others may respond positively. And as budding friendships grow, it is natural to want to spend time together.

> Friendship is born at that moment when one man says to another: "What! You too? I thought that no one but myself . . ."
>
> —C.S. Lewis

Extending a friendship beyond the workplace can present dilemmas. Take the issue of time, for example. The thought of adding one more activity to an overflowing schedule may seem daunting, but it need not.

Instead of adding something new to our calendars, we can look for common ground—an area where our lives overlap—where we can do something together, instead of doing it independently. Identifying common ground may be an indication that God is calling us to invest further in individuals.

> Yes, whatever a person is like, I try to find common ground with him so that he will let me tell him about Christ and let Christ save him.
>
> —1 Corinthians 9:22 (LB)

Common Interests

As we get to know people, we can watch for those who share our interests, such as:

- a particular sport or sports team
- antiquing
- genealogy
- fitness and nutrition
- gourmet cooking
- interior design
- an author or genre of literature
- animals
- politics
- community service
- woodworking
- a type of music, a recording artist, or band

Bill's Experience
I love fly-fishing. When I have a friend along to share the experience, it is even better. Talking about the Creator when surrounded by His beautiful creation can lead to meaningful conversation after a long day on the river.

Walt's Experience
Over the years, I developed hobbies by intentionally learning about topics of interest from nonbelievers. Getting involved in bird-watching, growing orchids, and Rotary Club has created opportunities to deepen relationships with nonbelievers.

Common Needs

As relationships with nonbelievers grow, it is important to remember that friendship should be reciprocal in nature. Allowing others to help us in some way can deepen friendships. And when we ask for assistance, this indicates that we value the gifts and wisdom of others.

> ### Walt's Experience
>
> For years, I thought the way into a person's life was always to be on the giving end. But I learned that when I allow people to help me, they become vested in me.
>
> My wife, Barb, and I were devastated to learn our first child had cerebral palsy (damage to the brain had occurred before she was born). The resulting delays in Kate's physical and mental development required Barb and me to seek out a number of folks—most were nonbelievers—to help us out. These prolonged relationships allowed us to cultivate and to plant spiritual seeds.

CONTACT WITHOUT CONTAMINATION

All of us can be tempted to rationalize activities or behavior for the sake of maintaining a relationship. C. S. Lewis wisely warned, "No clever arrangement of bad eggs ever made a good omelet."

As friendships grow, nonbelievers may invite us into their world, just as we have invited them into ours. This is an important step of openness, but it comes with a warning label: The lifestyle of many nonbelievers will likely include activities and conversation that may be either tempting or offensive to us.

Although some nonbelievers may be more moral and ethical than some believers, the lifestyle of most nonbelievers will likely include activities and conversation that can be either tempting or offensive to us.

Even the most devoted Christians can be tempted to do something they know is wrong. For example, a Christian who has struggles with alcohol may need to graciously say no when invited to join a group of colleagues for a drink after work.

When developing common ground with nonbelieving colleagues of the opposite sex, special care should be taken. In his letter to Timothy, Paul warns, "Flee the evil desires of youth, and pursue righteousness, faith, love and peace, along with those who call on the Lord out of a pure heart" (2 Tim. 2:22).

> **Bill's Experience**
> A Christian friend of mine asked a nonbelieving female friend if he could help her move from one apartment to another. He had a truck, and he figured this would be an excellent opportunity to serve her and pave the way for conversations about faith. As they unloaded the last piece of furniture, she offered to return the favor—sexually. He wisely left immediately, which made his friend angry. He may have burned a bridge to the relationship, but he maintained his integrity.

If we succumb to temptation and join unbelievers in activities the Bible says are sinful, we lose our saltiness and are "no longer good for anything except to be thrown out and trampled underfoot by men."[11] On the other hand, if we respond too negatively, we may damage a relationship.

Facing Offensive Behavior Inoffensively

So, how do we make contact with nonbelievers without alienating them unnecessarily or becoming contaminated? Paul provides the answer: In relationships with nonbelievers, wisdom is paramount.

> To be a Christian means to forgive the inexcusable because God has forgiven the inexcusable in you.
> —C.S. Lewis

> Be wise in the way you act toward outsiders; make the most of every opportunity. Let your conversation be always full of grace, seasoned with salt, so that you may know how to answer everyone.
> —Colossians 4:5-6

Given Paul's counsel, the following wisdom can guide our thoughts and actions:

Do not be surprised at people's sinfulness. It is always a good practice to think the best of others, but we should not forget that nonbelievers are under the dominion of Satan.[12] Without Christ, they are spiritually dead and held captive by the devil to do his will.[13] Until they find fulfillment in Christ, they will seek it elsewhere, sometimes in extremely dark places.

Put the Holy Spirit in charge of cleanup. Although we should not excuse bad behavior, confronting people's sinfulness is usually counterproductive. Conviction is not our responsibility. Jesus gave that job to the Holy Spirit.[14] When we try to induce conviction, it is far less persuasive—and we come across as arrogant and judgmental. When the apostle Paul entered a city where the culture was decadent, he did not preach to nonbelievers about their moral depravity. He offered a relationship with God through Jesus, a relationship that could change the core of their being.

Make choices based on truth, not opinion. Believers differ on what is acceptable and unacceptable behavior. According to Paul, however, we have no right to impose our convictions on others. We should evaluate and set our boundaries by God's Word, not someone's lists of acceptable and unacceptable behavior.[15]

Say No with Grace

When someone invites us to participate in questionable or offensive activities, we need not be belligerent or defensive. We can turn down such offers gracefully, using these guidelines:

> You don't always have to chop with the sword of truth. You can point with it, too.
> —Anne Lamott

Take into account the intent of the invitation. When nonbelievers invite us to participate in activities we consider sinful, in all likelihood they are not trying to tempt us to sin. They simply want to share something they enjoy. Their intention can be positive, even if the suggested action is not.

However, if we sense that they are using the invitation as a test or trap of some sort, we should simply say that we are not comfortable engaging in the activity.

Offer an acceptable alternative. If an invitation is one of genuine friendship, the person may simply want to spend time with us. By suggesting another option, we keep the door open and affirm our appreciation.

> **Walt's Experience**
> Some nonbelieving friends invited Barb and me to a movie we felt would be wrong for us to attend. Rather than making a big deal about it, I said, "We'd love to go to the movies with you, but Barb has really wanted to see _____ [I named another movie]. Have you seen it yet? We've heard that it's great."
>
> It turned out they just wanted to spend an evening with us, and they didn't care what movie we saw. Later that night over coffee, we discussed the movie and some spiritual implications of the plot.

Watch the excuses. Today, Christians in America are defined more by what we don't do than by what we do. We should try to avoid pointing to God as the reason for not participating—unless we are forced to do so by a direct challenge to our faith.

EXTENDING GRACE

God's love and grace, not His judgment, drew each of us to Him. He went out of His way to seek a relationship with us, despite our repulsiveness. We can show our gratitude by being gracious to others. When we needlessly distance ourselves from nonbelievers, it is reasonable to ask why someone would want a relationship with us—or our God.

> Don't just throw the seed at the people! Grind it into flour, bake it into bread, and slice it for them. And it wouldn't hurt to put a little honey on it.
> – Charles Spurgeon

However, when we are "wise in the way we act toward outsiders" and our conversation is "full of grace, seasoned with salt," we can build relationships that the Holy Spirit can use to prepare hearts for a relationship with our Savior.

The Bottom Line

Jesus calls us salt of the earth. For salt to make a difference, it has to make contact.

Planting

But how can they call on him to save them
unless they believe in him?
And how can they believe in him
if they have never heard about him?
And how can they hear about him
unless someone tells them?
—Romans 10:14 (NLT)

Chapter 9

Walking Through Open Doors

"You never know till you try to reach them how accessible men are;
but you must approach each man by the right door."
—*Henry Ward Beecher*

S ometimes, people who attend "*Workplace Grace*"
seminars question our emphasis on the cultivation stage of
evangelism. They are eager to plant, so they can get to the
harvesting stage. And the sooner, the better!

The answer is always the same: Whether we are
cultivating a field to plant cotton seeds or a heart to plant gospel seeds,
the more time, energy, and prayer we put into preparing soil conditions
for optimum growth, the more likely the harvest will be fruitful.
Cultivation, however, is never an end in itself. We cultivate so we can
plant, and we plant to produce a harvest.

Quick review: Since salvation is God's work, our first step in
evangelism is to discern where the Holy Spirit is working in an
individual's life, and join Him at that place. God uses us to cultivate
heart soil, plant seeds of truth, and help our coworkers and friends take
steps toward a saving relationship with Christ. And, sometimes, we get
to participate in the harvest.

A nonbeliever's heart softens and becomes more receptive to the gospel as emotional barriers decrease, and trust in us—in who we are and what we say—increases. But we should not be surprised when people with whom we have been building relationships begin to raise legitimate questions about spiritual topics. Their questions typically signal that heart soil is ready for planting to begin. While watching for opportunities to communicate seeds of biblical truth, we should keep three things in mind:

> Questions typically signal that heart soil is ready for planting to begin.

1. The boundary between cultivating and planting is not hard and fast. As we begin to plant, we continue to cultivate relationships and build trust.

2. The planting stage involves much more than a one-time explanation of the gospel. During this stage, we help people address sincere, well-founded, and, perhaps, long-standing intellectual questions about faith and Christianity.

3. As a nonbeliever moves closer to a personal relationship with Christ, resistance may increase. Satan often escalates the battle for a person's soul when he senses defeat close at hand.

> **Important**
> Although watching others make progress toward the most important decision in life is exciting, we must remember that the ongoing battle in the spiritual realm is intensifying.

SOIL ANALYSIS

In the Planting Phase, nonbelievers begin to view the Bible from a different perspective and consider how it might be personally relevant. The goal of this phase is not to win arguments but for nonbelievers to gain understanding.

When we scatter seeds of truth and nonbelievers begin to process what we say, questions naturally arise based on their perceptions of truth. Analysis of heart soil in this phase involves identifying and assessing intellectual barriers, which must be addressed before individuals can understand and embrace God's gift of eternal life.

An intellectual barrier typically presents as a predisposition to dismiss or reject Christianity. Upbringing, education, experiences, influential people, and sometimes all of the above have shaped the thinking of nonbelievers. They may view Christianity as false, irrelevant, or simply a social construct. Some, however, see Christianity as a dangerous threat.

> It ain't those parts of the Bible that I can't understand that bother me, it is the parts that I do understand.
>
> —Mark Twain

Intellectual barriers usually stem from misconceptions about the Christian faith and lack of firsthand knowledge of the Bible. Many people perceive Christianity as a performance-based religion with a boatload of heavy-handed, guilt-inducing rules that make life unpleasant.

Performance mentality stems in part from our innate desire to prove ourselves worthy of God's love and attention. Religious organizations and churches sometimes feed this proclivity by stressing what people should do for the organization rather than what God wants to do for them personally. As a result, when we talk about faith, some people may assume that we are talking about additional obligations or oppressive responsibilities. Small wonder they are not interested! They have never considered what God promises to do for them, as well as the Bible's relevance for their lives.

Intellectual barriers usually stem from misconceptions about the Christian faith and lack of firsthand knowledge of the Bible.

Soil Treatment

The true essence of the Christian faith is radically different than the perception of most nonbelievers. Christianity is primarily about what *God has done* for us, not what *we do* for Him. It is not about how we qualify for membership or acceptance, nor is it about cleaning up our lives before He will accept us. It is about experiencing the abundant life in an intensely personal, loving relationship with our Creator, which is made possible by the sacrifice of Jesus.

Nonbelievers need to understand who Jesus is and what He has done for us—and they need to see Jesus' life lived out in us. They also need a nonthreatening environment to investigate what the Bible says, to wrestle with its plausibility, and to consider its relevance for life. As we offer thoughtful answers to their questions and respond respectfully to their challenges, God can use us to change their thinking about Christ. This usually happens over a period of time.

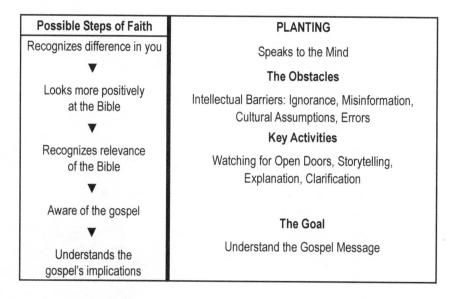

Possible Steps of Faith	PLANTING
Recognizes difference in you	Speaks to the Mind
▼	
Looks more positively at the Bible	**The Obstacles**
	Intellectual Barriers: Ignorance, Misinformation, Cultural Assumptions, Errors
▼	**Key Activities**
Recognizes relevance of the Bible	Watching for Open Doors, Storytelling, Explanation, Clarification
▼	
Aware of the gospel	**The Goal**
▼	Understand the Gospel Message
Understands the gospel's implications	

How to Recognize Open Doors

In his letter to the Colossian church, Paul uses an open door metaphor. He writes, "And pray for us, too, that God may open a door for our message, so that we may proclaim the mystery of Christ, for which I am in chains" (Col. 4:3).

In evangelism, an open door is an invitation to enter the conference room of a person's mind to discuss a spiritual issue or question. As we watch for opportunities to bring faith into a discussion, it is helpful to envision someone opening or closing the door of his or her mind in the same way one might open or close a physical door. When we knock, it is up to our colleague to open the door. This is always the result of the Holy Spirit's work.

A door remains open only as long as a nonbeliever wants to continue the conversation. As with any conversation, it is important to be sensitive to verbal and nonverbal cues that suggest the person is becoming uncomfortable. This means the door is closing. Trying to push the door back open may damage the relationship and reinforce existing barriers to the gospel.

Consider Jesus' conversation with the Samaritan woman.[1] Jesus did not confront her as he did Nicodemus.[2] He knocked on the door and she cautiously opened it. But notice that Jesus did not barge in. He offered bits of spiritual truth, one at a time, and then waited for her response, allowing her to determine if she wanted to continue talking. She could have stopped the conversation at any point, but with each comment of Jesus, she opened the door wider.

> The Holy Spirit and His operation upon us are absolutely essential before we can receive the truth or begin to understand it.
> —Martyn Lloyd-Jones

Sometimes, a nonbeliever will swing the door open wide for conversation with a question or request. Other times, it may not be obvious if the welcome mat is out. Two things can help clarify:

1. Listen for expressions of felt needs. We should be alert for mentions of challenges or concerns, such as health issues, a parenting challenge, or angst about a business problem. Speaking openly about

> When people talk, listen completely. Most people never listen.
> —Ernest Hemingway

such struggles can indicate the individual is looking for meaningful answers to life's problems.

2. Ask questions and actively listen to responses. If the door appears cracked, but we are uncertain, we can ask questions that show our interest in a person's life, sticking to safe topics related to things already mentioned in conversation. Some questions can lead to a natural place to bring up faith in a conversation: "How's your daughter doing?" "What's happening with that situation with your client?" Based on the response, we can gently expand on the topic of faith or move onto something else.

> You cannot truly listen to anyone and do anything else at the same time.
> —M. Scott Peck

Walking Through an Open Door

When someone opens a door, we should keep the following guidelines in mind:

- ▶ **Proceed slowly.** We should resist the temptation to rush in and offer advice or try to fix a coworker's problems. Planting seeds is about dialogue, not fixing, teaching, or preaching. We must be alert for the Spirit's guidance, and watch our pace.

> Many people seek a sympathetic ear and do not find it among the Christians, because these Christians are talking even when they should be listening.
>
> —Dietrich Bonhoeffer

- ▶ **Ask permission to speak further.** We can broach most any subject (including religion), if we ask permission and speak with respect and sensitivity. For example, "May I share something I've learned about that?" or "May I tell you a story about something that helped me with a similar problem?" A nod from the listener usually indicates an open door.

▶ **Avoid religious jargon.** Listeners may not understand certain words and phrases that are familiar to Christians, such as:

- The Lord was working in my heart.
- During my quiet time
- Lost sheep, straying from the fold
- A time of communion and fellowship
- Hedge of protection
- Let me share my testimony with you.
- I have a burden on my heart.

To admit their ignorance by asking for clarification could prove embarrassing and hinder communication.

▶ **Don't misjudge the listener's discomfort.** Uneasiness about a spiritual topic is not always the reason a door begins to close. The listener may feel pressure about an upcoming meeting or deadline, or remember something unrelated to your conversation that produces angst. Suggesting another time to continue talking (before work, at lunch, or after work) demonstrates respect and sensitivity.

▶ **Track together.** Good communication means both the speaker and the listener understand what the other is saying. Asking for clarification when a coworker makes a statement is always appropriate: "I'm not sure I got that. Can you explain it a bit more?" When we are unsure if someone understands what we've said, we can simply ask, "Am I making sense?"

▶ **Regulate the dosage.** We should offer small bites of truth and let the Holy Spirit help with digestion. It is more effective to pique interest and leave people wanting more rather than to overpower them with more information than they can process.

▶ **Don't react negatively to objections.** Although emotional obstacles, such as anger and hostility toward Christianity, are common in the cultivation phase of evangelism, sometimes they resurface during the planting phase.

▶ **Coworkers may have grown to trust us, but certain topics of conversation may remind them of unpleasant experiences.** We should recognize and appreciate emotions, and not take it personally. An ungracious response can undo months of building trust.

> The heart of the godly thinks carefully before speaking.
> —Proverbs 15:28 (NLT)

▶ **Ask God for help.** In the midst of a conversation that is heating up, we can silently pray and ask God to give us discipline not to react and wisdom to respond with grace and truth.

TELLING OUR STORY

An effective way to convey spiritual truth and basics of the gospel message is to tell the story of our personal spiritual journey, and how Christ has enriched our life and our relationships with others. As followers of Jesus, each of us should all be able and ready to tell our own faith story in a clear and compelling way.

As followers of Jesus, each of us should all be able and ready to tell our own faith story in a clear and compelling way.

It is often helpful to create an outline or timeline of defining moments along our journey to faith. Once the framework is in place, details can be added. Some may choose to start writing out the story word for word, like a memoir, and later edit as needed.

A Biblical Example

When Paul stood before King Agrippa and his court, he spoke simply and clearly about how Jesus had changed his life.[3] Paul presented his testimony succinctly and in what appears to be a conversational tone. His presentation provides a practical template for telling our own story. Paul included the following:

- ► brief introduction

- ► summary of his life before he met Jesus

- ► description of how he met Jesus

- ► summary of his life after he met Jesus

Here are some helpful guidelines:

1. Use conversational language. No one wants to hear a story that sounds like a term paper. Using words we naturally use in the course of everyday conversations is the best approach. For example:

I've always tended to be a people pleaser, and this really got me into trouble when I landed my first job. Whatever my boss asked me to jump, I asked, "How high?"

I consistently overpromised what I could realistically do and had to stay later and later at work to make it happen. I had no life outside of work—except for when I'd stop at a local bar before going home to crash for a few hours. I felt like a squirrel trapped in a cage, and I didn't know how to get out.

2. Tell the story without preaching. We should never use our stories to give advice about someone else's problem. For example:

I used to be depressed a lot before I became a Christian, so I understand firsthand what you're dealing with. You should try this class at my church for people with depression. I think it would really help you.

3. Avoid details that are unnecessary to the story, specifically those that could have a negative connotation. We should tell our stories without mentioning the names of pastors, churches, denominations, or political organizations—any of which could raise a red flag. We should also avoid specific dates, ages, or locations that are not relevant and could color the listener's perception. For example:

God started working in my life when I was about your age. I was eating lunch with my friend, Buzz, at The Pit—best barbeque in town. The owners support "Save the Cedars" day, so I like to give them my business.

Anyway, Buzz was a deacon down at First Baptist, and I knew he was close with God. I'd been feeling down since my first wife left earlier that year, so I wondered if God could help. Buzz told me what the Bible had to say about my loneliness and invited me to church.

4. Include human interest or a humorous touch. Interesting facts draw people in, and humor can be disarming A story that touches real life or makes people laugh can reduce tension and increase attention. It allows listeners to drop their defenses and look beyond obstacles. For example:

For the first time in my life, I experienced real joy. I don't think anyone at the office knew how unhappy I was. I had become an expert at covering up my tears—as well as my grey hair.

5. Explain the gospel briefly. Our own stories should lead in a natural, unforced way to explaining the basic facts of the gospel. For example:

I was seven months pregnant with our first child when we moved cross-country. My husband traveled a lot, and I missed my friends. I was in a really dark place, without hope. I was scared about having a baby and scared about the future. I didn't know where to turn.

As I stared at all the unpacked boxes, I remembered seeing a Bible in our realtor's car. She told me to call her if I ever needed anything. I desperately needed someone to talk to, so I called her. She came by the house later that day, and I poured out my heart.

She listened, cried with me, and then asked if she could tell me what gives her hope. As I listened, I learned that God created me for a purpose, He knows me better than I know myself, and He loves me more than I can comprehend. I thought of all the things I had done that made me want to hide from God.

Then, for the first time, I understood why Jesus came. He stood in my place and took the punishment I deserved for all the bad things I'd done. His death paid the penalty for every one of them. I realized that Jesus is stronger than death itself because He rose to life again— eternal life—and He wants to help me live life today and give me eternal life too. That day, I believed and my friend helped me pray. I thanked God for all He has done for me. I told Him how sorry I was for ignoring Him, I accepted His gift of salvation and gave Him my life. I told Him I was ready for Him to run things since I wasn't doing such a good job.

6. Explain how God meets our deepest inner needs. We can describe how Christians can experience a deep sense of joy, peace, hope, and satisfaction, but we should avoid giving the impression that the Christian life is all blue sky and green lights—because it is not. For example:

> We should avoid giving the impression that the Christian life is all blue sky and green lights.

Since I became a follower of Christ, my problems haven't gone away. But God gives me strength and wisdom for how to deal with them. He has given me a sense of peace and a new perspective about life and my purpose for being here.

7. Don't expect to write it in one sitting. The more complex the story, the more thought will be required to create a clear and concise presentation. As we organize the details and shape our stories, we should ask ourselves questions during the process:

▶ What parts are most relevant to the nonbelievers I know?

▶ Are there instances that are inappropriate to mention in detail, as they might embarrass the listener or dishonor those who played a role in dark parts of my life?

▶ How can I tailor my story to the age, stage of life, and present circumstances of my listener?

▶ What parts of my story can I mention that might open the door for more spiritual discussion?

Most importantly, we should pray that God will allow His word to penetrate the hearts of those who hear our stories. The Word of God is powerful, and God will speak through His word to anyone who comes with a seeker's heart.

8. Practice. When we feel comfortable with the facts and flow of our stories, we should practice telling them to Christian friends. Their feedback will help us make our personal stories clearer and more concise. Each of us should continue to practice telling our story until the order and words feel comfortable and familiar, but not memorized verbatim. A rote presentation is likely to come across as canned and insincere.

The Bottom Line

When a door opens for planting seeds of truth, walk through wisely. If it closes, don't try to open a window. Wait on God's timing. He is at work.

Chapter 10

The Whole Truth

I seemed to hear God saying, "Put down your gun and we'll talk."
—C.S. Lewis

The role of ambassadors is to represent the interests and priorities of their countries, taking into account the customs and cultural sensitivities of the foreign nations to which they are sent.

One characteristic separates highly effective ambassadors from those who are not successful in their roles: the ability to communicate well.

> The traditional image of an ambassador as a highly polished individual who is so circumspect in what he says that it requires a special talent to figure out what he is saying is incorrect. Articulateness in explaining, reporting, defending, and discussing information on his country's position and other matters is essential.[1]

AMBASSADORS OF THE KING

In like manner, we are ambassadors of the King of the Universe, representing His interests and priorities. In Paul's second letter to disciples in Corinth, he wrote, "We are therefore Christ's ambassadors, as though God were making his appeal through us. We implore you on Christ's behalf: Be reconciled to God" (2 Cor. 5:20).

127

Paul says that God is pleading through us. He uses our words as the means through which nonbelievers receive the message of reconciliation. To fulfill our role as effective ambassadors, we must communicate God's message in a clear, concise way that connects the gospel to the unique needs, life context, and worldview of each nonbeliever.

MOTIVATIONS TO BELIEVE

The heart of the gospel is Christ's substitutionary death and bodily resurrection. He died in our place, taking the punishment we deserve, so we could be reconciled with God. He rose from the dead, securing eternal life for all who trust in Him.

> Now, brothers and sisters, I want to remind you of the gospel I preached to you ... That Christ died for our sins according to the Scriptures, that he was buried, that he was raised on the third day according to the Scriptures.
>
> —1 Corinthians 15:1-4

However, whether we long to be loved unconditionally, feel shameful about behaviors we know are sinful, or fear what happens when we die, we place our trust in Christ because we sense a need only He can meet. When we present the gospel message to others, it is important to understand each person's deepest longings and connect particular benefits of the gospel to those needs.

> Truth should not be simply declared into a vacuum—it must be delivered as a response to the questions of particular people.
> —Tim Keller

In his book, *Center Church* (Zondervan), Tim Keller suggests a number of motivations that create openness to the gospel.[2] The following six are adapted from his list.

1. Fear of Judgment and Death

Since mankind's first rebellious act, fear has plagued our race.[3] The Bible tells us that God's perfect love delivers us from the fear of judgment[4] and death.[5]

2. Guilt and Shame

Because we cannot live up to our own standards, much less God's, we live under the burden of guilt and shame apart from Christ. But God declares us "not guilty" through Christ's redemption,[6] and we can come before Him boldly with a clear conscience.[7]

> **Bill's Experience**
> When I was growing up, I spent lots of time at church, so words like guilt, sin, heaven, and hell were familiar ones. I had no argument with the fact that I was a sinner. I knew that my sin created a problem between God and me. I wanted to be forgiven. I just didn't know how to make things right. I heard the gospel more times than I can count, and I understood in my head that Jesus died for the sins of the world. But I had no idea what that meant to me.
>
> The presentation of the gospel that finally got my attention explained that Jesus died for Bill Peel, in my place. He took my personal sin upon Himself so I could be forgiven. I wanted all of that I could get.

3. Attractiveness of the Truth

We cope with inconsistencies in our worldview until our experience forces us to confront them (the existence of evil and suffering, for example). The gospel offers an internally consistent worldview that explains reality.[8] In Acts 17, Paul used this approach in Athens when he confronted the inconsistency of the Athenian's belief system.

> The gospel offers an internally consistent worldview that explains reality.

4. Help with a Problem

At some point, we all face problems that money, connections, and personal power cannot solve. When we run out of solutions, Jesus does not hesitate to help those who come to Him in faith.[9]

5. Love and Acceptance

We all hunger for love and acceptance—things the world cannot deliver to our satisfaction. Jesus restores our relationship with God, who loves and accepts us more than we ever dreamed possible, although we are more sinful than we ever dare imagine.[10]

6. Adequacy and Significance

> As people designed by God to rule creation, we long for the power and position lost in the fall.

As people designed by God to rule creation, we long for the power and position lost in the fall.[11] We hunger to feel adequate and significant. In Christ, our standing is restored as heirs of the King,[12] and we have the ability to live the life for which we were created.[13]

EXPLAINING KEY POINTS OF THE GOSPEL

Communicating the gospel with clarity is important when we sense an open door. Paul himself asked for prayer about clear communication.

> And pray for us, too, that God may open a door for our message, so that we may proclaim the mystery of Christ, for which I am in chains. Pray that I may proclaim it clearly, as I should. (Col. 4:3-4)

A clear gospel message answers seven basic questions. Listeners need at least a rudimentary understanding of what the Bible teaches about these issues in order to respond to the gospel.

1. Who is God?

Three things are important to understand.

▶ **God is Creator and Ruler.** The Bible tells us that the universe is not an accident. It was created by an all-powerful God. As the Creator, He rightfully rules over all creation. He is the source of all life, and everyone and everything exists at His pleasure, making His will and judgment absolute and inescapable.[14]

▶ **God is loving.** Love is an essential attribute of the God of the Bible, not something tangential to His being. Because of this, He sought a way to reconcile to Himself creatures who disregarded His authority.

▶ **God is compassionate.** Although God has every justification to bring judgment on anyone who would harm His creation, the first attribute God ascribes to Himself is compassionate.[15] He feels our pain and is sympathetic to our condition.

> What comes into our minds when we think about God is the most important thing about us.
>
> —A. W. Tozer

2. Who are we?

God created human beings in His image to:

▶ **Live in relationship.** God created us to live in harmony with Him and each other in the paradise He created.

> And out of that hopeless attempt has come nearly all that we call human history—money, poverty, ambition, war, prostitution, classes, empires, slavery—the long terrible story of man trying to find something other than God which will make him happy.
>
> —C.S. Lewis, *Mere Christianity*

▶ **Join His work.** God invited us to work as co-creators. He empowered us to rule the world and develop creation into all He intended.

3. What happened?

The evil, pain, and suffering in the world are not God's doing. They are the result of a decision made by the first representatives of our race who doubted His love and disregarded His rightful authority.

- ▶ **They doubted God's goodness.** They decided they knew best, and chose to do life their way.

- ▶ **They chose to meet their needs apart of God.** They became takers rather than givers and tried to write God out of our story. This is what the Bible means when it talks about sin. It is not about religious rules, but the breaking of a relationship with the Source of Life.

- ▶ **They suffered the consequences of their choices.** To paraphrase C. S. Lewis, when man failed to say, "Thy will be done" to God, God said "Thy will be done" to man, allowing us to taste and see the consequences of this choice. As a result of sin, every human is born spiritually dead, cut off from God's power and presence.

Alienated from God, everything came unraveled.

- ▶ **Perfect peace** was exchanged for personal and interpersonal conflict and war.

- ▶ **Prosperity** was replaced by hunger, poverty, injustice, racism, and bitterness.

> The gospel is good news about what Jesus Christ has done to restore our relationship with God.

- ▶ **Purpose** gave way to meaninglessness and despair.

- ▶ **Physical health** was displaced by sickness and physical death.

4. What did God do?

Because God is loving and gracious, He did not leave us to ourselves.

▶ **He intervened.** As an outpouring of His love and compassion,
He chose grace
rather than
judgment and put
a plan into action
to restore our relationship with Him. [16]

> Religion says, "I obey; therefore, I am accepted."
>
> The gospel says, "I am accepted; therefore, I obey."

▶ **He sent Jesus.** God the Father sent God the Son who laid
aside His divine privileges and came to earth—becoming fully
human without diminishing His deity—in the person of Jesus
Christ, to live, die, and rise to life again so He could restore us
to Himself.[17]

5. What did Jesus do?

John explains the greatest event in human history: "The Word became
flesh and made his dwelling among us. We have seen his glory, the
glory of the One and Only, who came from the Father, full of grace and
truth" (John 1:14).

▶ **Jesus lived the life we should have lived.** He came to earth to
show us who God is and how He intended us to live.[18] He lived a
perfect, sinless life, always doing the Father's will.

▶ **Jesus died the death we should have died.** As an act of sheer
grace, He subjected Himself to the divine justice and judgment,
taking our sin upon Himself and dying in our place.[19]

▶ **He rose from the dead that we might live.** Through Christ
alone, we have eternal life.[20]

6. How do we respond?

Christianity is different than other religions that require people to
redeem themselves through self-effort and good works. The gospel
requires simply that we...

▶ **Believe.** To believe means to trust, to place our faith in, to wholly rely on. When we believe, we turn from our commitment to define our own lives and save ourselves, and, instead, depend wholly on Christ's work—His death and resurrection—to restore us to life and fellowship with God.[21]

▶ **Receive.** Salvation is a gift given freely to all who are willing to receive it. The gospel is not about what we do, but what God has done for us. That is good news, since we are powerless to live the life God intended.

> To be "in Christ" is to place one's trust in Him for salvation from sin. To be "in Christ" is to trust His goodness, not our own; to trust that His sacrificial death on the cross paid the complete debt of death we owe for our sin; to trust that His resurrection gives us eternal life instead of relying upon our own ability to please God. To be "in Christ" is to claim, by faith, the free gift of salvation. To be "in Christ" is to enjoy a completely restored relationship with our Father in heaven by virtue of His Son's righteous standing.
>
> —Charles R. Swindoll

7. What does God promise to those who believe?

God promises to forgive our sin, give us eternal life, and make us part of His family.[22]

He does not promise to remove our problems, but He does promise to strengthen us as we face them.[23]

He does not take away our propensity to act sinfully, but He gives us a new life and the ability to renew our minds, resist temptation, choose obedience, and live lives of meaning and purpose.[24]

PREPARED TO SPEAK THE TRUTH

We never want to pick green fruit, but neither do we want to neglect the harvest when fruit is ripe. Because God is always at work, we should always be prepared to share the gospel with a hungry soul.

> "We are not called to proclaim philosophy and metaphysics, but the simple gospel. Man's fall, his need of a new birth, forgiveness through atonement, and salvation as the result of faith, these are our battle-ax and weapons of war."
>
> —Charles Spurgeon

The Gospel in One Verse

Although gospel tracts have their place in the Planting Phase, it is more natural and comfortable if we are able to create our own tract, so to speak, by sketching a simple diagram. This gives us the flexibility to create a visual of the gospel anywhere, using a scrap of paper or napkin.

Here's an example of what this might look like, using Romans 6:23 to illustrate how Jesus' substitutionary death bridges the gap between God and man. (To watch a video demonstration, visit *www. CenterForFaithAndWork.com/Gospel-in-One-Verse*.)

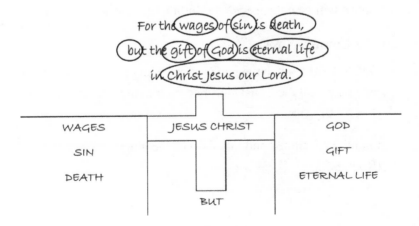

Romans 6:23 and John 3:16[25] provide an outline for a gospel discussion. This approach can take as little as five minutes, or it can be expanded as time and the interest of a listener allow.

Use the words of the verse as an outline.

Using Romans 6:23 as an example, we circle the word in the text that we want to explain, add it to our diagram, and explain how it relates to a particular aspect of the gospel message. For example, when we circle the word *death*, we explain that the verse is talking about more that physical death. It is also about spiritual death, separation from God, and all that this entails. Then we move on the next word, and the next, making our way through the entire verse, discussing key points along the way.

The Gospel in Your Mind

It is a good idea to memorize key verses. Chuck Swindoll wrote,

> I know of no other single practice in the Christian life more rewarding, practically speaking, than memorizing Scripture…No other single exercise pays greater spiritual dividends! Your prayer life will be strengthened. Your witnessing will be sharper and much more effective. Your attitudes and outlook will begin to change. Your mind will become alert and observant. Your confidence and assurance will be enhanced. Your faith will be solidified.[26]

Sin and Its Consequences

- ▶ We all, like sheep, have gone astray, each of us has turned to his own way; and the LORD has laid on him the iniquity of us all. (Isa. 53:6)

- ▶ For all have sinned and fall short of the glory of God. (Rom. 6:23)

Jesus' Sacrifice

- But God demonstrates his own love for us in this: While we were still sinners, Christ died for us. (Rom. 5:8)

- For Christ died for sins once for all, the righteous for the unrighteous, to bring you to God. (1 Pet. 3:18)

- As far as the east is from the west, so far has [the LORD] removed our transgressions from us." (Psalm 103:12)

Eternal Life

- Now this is eternal life: that they know you, the only true God, and Jesus Christ, whom you have sent. (John 17:4)

- And this is the testimony: God has given us eternal life, and this life is in his Son. He who has the Son has life; he who does not have the Son of God does not have life. I write these things to you who believe in the name of the Son of God so that you may know that you have eternal life." (1 John 5:11–13)

- For I am convinced that neither death nor life, neither angels nor demons, neither the present nor the future, nor any powers, neither height nor depth, nor anything else in all creation, will be able to separate us from the love of God that is in Christ Jesus our Lord." (Rom. 8:38–39)

No Bible handy? No problem. Numerous websites and mobile Apps offer the Bible online.
- Biblegateway.com website and Bible App
- Bible.org website and Bible App
- YouVersion website and Bible App

THE JOY OF THE HARVEST

In John 4, the disciples returned from the market in Sychar with lunch and were preoccupied with hunger. Jesus, however, had something else on His mind. He had planted seeds of truth in receptive heart soil, and it was time to reap the harvest.

On that day, Jesus and His disciples, as well as the Samaritan woman, all experienced the joy of seeing many people believe and become part of God's family.

> Many of the Samaritans from that town believed in him because of the woman's testimony ... And because of his words many more became believers.
>
> —John 4:39–41

Witnessing a new birth—whether physical or spiritual—is thrilling. And when we witness a new spiritual birth, we can know that all of heaven is rejoicing with us.[27] Some of our most precious memories in life will be seeing coworkers and friends come to Jesus.

The Bottom Line

To be effective ambassadors for Christ, we should learn to communicate the gospel in a clear, concise way that connects to the felt needs of the listener.

Chapter 11

Facing Objections

The very man who has argued you down, will sometimes be found, years later, to have been influenced by what you said.

—*C. S. Lewis*

Imagine this scenario: God puts a nonbelieving coworker on your heart. You pray, strike up brief conversations, and identify some common interests. Over the next few months, you show interest in what your coworker deems important and watch for opportunities to demonstrate care and concern.

Your coworker invites you to a gathering after work and introduces you as a "friend and colleague." You say to yourself, *This is good! Trust and friendship are growing.*

One day, you see a natural opportunity to drop a Faith Flag, and you say, "After work, I'm serving dinner at a homeless shelter with some friends from church." Your coworker responds, "That's cool. I'd like to do that sometime."

You sense a door is opening to broach the topic of faith, and over lunch one day you tell your personal Faith Story. The response, however, is not what you expected. With an expression midway between puzzled and put out, your coworker remarks, "That's great that you found God, but millions of other people in other religions have found God too. How can Christians be so pompous to think that only *they* get to go to heaven? I didn't peg you as such an exclusive kind of person."

How would you reply?

PLANTING COMES WITH A WARNING

The Planting Phase of evangelism is about scattering seeds of truth in heart soil that has been cultivated and softened. But this stage comes with a warning: truth is often discomforting. When we engage in conversations about spiritual issues, others may object to things we say and become irritable or defensive. Their objections may be to the gospel itself, a specific tenet of the Christian faith, or a delicate moral issue such as abortion, homosexuality, or physician-assisted suicide. Whatever their issue and tone, we should treat them in a manner worthy of Christ.

Sometimes, that is easier said than done. Strong feelings about our own beliefs can provoke us to seek victory at all costs. Caught up in winning the battle, we can forget that winning the war is more important. The door will likely close for future discussion if we let our emotions rule when responding to objections.

> In all debates, let truth be thy aim, not victory or an unjust interest.
> —William Penn

We must remember that Jesus is not only concerned about truth; He is concerned about people. He loves people, and He wants us to love them too—even when they are belligerent and hard to love.

> Do not waste time bothering whether you "love" your neighbor; act as if you did. As soon as we do this, we find one of the great secrets. When you are behaving as if you loved someone you will presently come to love him.
> —C.S. Lewis

Paul told the Christians in Ephesus to speak the truth in love,[1] and he explained what love looks like to the church at Corinth.

> Love is patient, love is kind and is not jealous; love does not brag and is not arrogant, does not act unbecomingly; it does not seek its own, is not provoked, does not take into account a wrong suffered, does not rejoice in unrighteousness, but rejoices with the truth; bears all things, believes all things, hopes all things, endures all things. (1 Cor. 13:4-8)

And James wrote this advice: "Everyone should be quick to listen, slow to speak and slow to become angry, for man's anger does not bring about the righteous life that God desires" (James 1:19–20).

Motives are Important

Something is wrong if being right is more important than helping people take steps toward Jesus. When nonbelieving friends raise objections, if we catch ourselves making statements similar to the following, we have lost sight of the main objective of the planting phase: sowing seeds of truth in a loving way.

- ► It's a proven fact that ...

- ► That's just the way it is.

- ► There's no question about ...

- ► Only fools believe ...

- ► You don't know what you're talking about.

- ► That's ridiculous.

- ► Just look at the evidence!

- ► That just doesn't fit the facts.

- ► You're not serious!

- ► Well, if you believe that, then ...

- There's just no evidence for ...

- Give me a break; that's been entirely disproved.

- You're committing intellectual suicide.

- You're totally illogical.

- How can you even say that?

Such responses can come across as a personal attack, causing others to react defensively and emotionally. When this happens, we must remember that nonbelieving coworkers are not the enemy; they are captives of the Enemy. Our job is to win friends by demonstrating love as we seek to help them find the truth.

Here are some ways to respectfully express disagreement, while affirming the value of the individual and keeping the door open for further discussion:[2]

- I hear what you're saying, but that does raise a red flag for me.

- My perspective is a little different. May I share it with you?

- Correct me if I'm wrong, but I see a conflict between ...

- I'm not piecing the facts together in the same way.

- That would make a lot of sense to me, but ...

- I agree with you concerning ... but I see the issue differently.

- I'm not sure I agree. Could I hear that again?

- Have you considered the evidence for ...?

- May I offer you another opinion?

Columbo and Socrates

We can learn a lot about people's motivations and the context of their objections from the method of the television character Columbo, a disheveled LAPD homicide detective.

Lieutenant Columbo, portrayed by the late Peter Falk, did not carry a gun. He drove a beat-up car and wore a rumpled raincoat, every day, rain or shine. Despite his unprofessional appearance, he always solved the case.

Columbo was a gumshoe Socrates. He simply asked questions and pondered the answers. Then he would ask more questions. He gently coaxed suspects to explain a case from their perspective and give their opinions about how the victim died. Over time, Columbo would whittle away at the logical inconsistencies in each suspect's story. He did not point out fallacies or accuse a suspect right away. Instead, he played dumb and continued to question puzzling details. The truth inevitably surfaced, allowing him to solve each case.

Socratic Evangelism

Responding to objections with Socratic-like questioning can help our nonbelieving friends recognize spiritual reality. Jesus often used well-turned questions to lead people to the truth without directly engaging them in debate.

Consider these examples:
One day, certain religious leaders who were trying to trap him asked, "Is it right to pay taxes to Caesar or not?" Jesus didn't answer the question. Instead he asked, "Whose portrait is this [on the coin]? And whose inscription?" (Matt. 22:17, 20)

Some of the religious leaders zeroed in on Sabbath observance: "Is it lawful to heal on the Sabbath?" Jesus replied, "If any of you has a sheep and it falls into a pit on the Sabbath, will you not take hold of it and lift it out? How much more valuable is a man than a sheep!" (Matt. 12:10–12)

> When Jesus was asked by a rich man, "Good teacher ... what must I do to inherit eternal life?" Jesus discerned the question's intent and responded with the question, "Why do you call me good?" (Mark 10:17–18)

The Value of a Good Question

Responding to an objection with a question asked in a humble, sincere tone has positive benefits.

- ▶ It tells nonbelievers we value their opinion. It opens the way for dialogue and curbs any tendencies we may have to throttle conversation with monologue.

- ▶ It fosters clear communication. A question such as, "Would you please explain what you mean by that?" can help sidestep misinterpretation or incorrect assumptions on our part.

- ▶ It encourages thoughtful evaluation. A question can gently nudge nonbelievers to consider what they believe. This may be a novel experience for those who have blindly embraced the beliefs of others without thinking them through. A good question allows people the opportunity to discover truth for themselves.

- ▶ It can help us better understand the issues nonbelievers have with Christianity. People may see us as a safe place to discuss past experiences that turned them against Christianity.

> **Walt's Experience**
> Phil was a college friend. After I became a Christian, we discussed and debated spiritual issues, but he rejected Jesus.
> Twenty years later, Phil and I had dinner. While he proudly declared his atheist worldview had not changed, he asked me to explain, from my Christian perspective, the role of disease in people's lives. I was tempted to teach. I knew the arguments and the data. But I sensed a gentle prompt from the Spirit saying, *Ask and listen.*

I breathed a prayer for wisdom and then asked, "Phil, from your viewpoint, how would you answer that question? How do you explain suffering?"

His eyes welled with tears before he responded, "Walt, I don't have an answer." I could tell the issue was a personal one. I asked if I could tell him a story, and he nodded assent.

I told him about the anger Barb and I felt when we discovered that our daughter Kate had severe brain damage. I told him about the lessons some Christian friends had taught us about disease and evil, and how our marriage and faith had grown stronger through those dark days. It was a tearful conversation for both of us, and gospel seeds were planted.

Though I don't see Phil often, when we get together, our times are special for both of us. Each visit he asks more questions, and so do I.

TURNING OBJECTIONS INTO OPPORTUNITIES

How we handle objections will determine if they turn into opportunities or obstacles on the path to belief in Christ. Although objections may feel like personal attacks, they may stem from unspoken misgivings, such as, *Do you really care about me and what I think? Are you like other critical Christians I've met? Do you have a reasonable answer, or are you going to try to persuade me with canned talking points?*

Answering objections is about exchanging viewpoints without damaging connections with our colleagues. We should keep the following guidelines in mind when others express doubt about what they are learning from us about the Christian faith.

▶ **Do not react negatively.**
It should be no surprise that people who do not know Jesus hold views that do not conform to the truth of Scripture. The gospel can be hard to swallow, and people often choke

> My greatest strength as a consultant is to be ignorant and ask a few questions.
>
> —Peter Drucker

on the truth when confronted with it. Nonbelievers have every right to expect us to respond to their honest objections—even emotionally charged ones—with respect and thoughtfulness.

► Be gracious and humble.

People who think they know everything are painful to be around. If our faith is secure and our identity is rooted in who we are in Christ, we have nothing to prove and can allow people to progress toward truth at their own pace.

Paul warned the Corinthian church, "Knowledge puffs up, but love builds up. The man who thinks he knows something does not yet know as he ought to know" (1 Cor. 8:1–2).

► Do not be discouraged.

All human beings, whether they realize it or not, have a hunger in their soul for God. If people are at least willing to talk with us about spiritual issues, even if they are posing objections, we can be thankful they are still shopping, even if not yet buying.

► Recognize the value of doubt.

> Our hearts are restless until they find rest in God.
> —St. Augustine

Doubt is often the doorway to faith. It may mean people are pondering truth. We should offer answers to their doubts, but also give them time to think.

► Use the Bible whenever possible.

Scripture is the most powerful tool we have. Our own thoughts and ideas can be relevant and hold sway, but God's Word is qualitatively different.

> The word of God is living and active. Sharper than any double-edged sword, it penetrates even to dividing soul and spirit, joints and marrow; it judges the thoughts and attitudes of the heart.
>
> —Hebrews 4:12

We should not, however, beat people over the head with the Bible. In fact, if we bring in Scripture prematurely, eyes may glaze over if people do not respect its authority. Christianity must become attractive to them, to the point that they think, *It would be wonderful it were true, but is it?* Only then will they consider listening to what the Bible says.

> Do not argue with those who are not ready. Do not browbeat them; do not insult them; do not try to high-pressure them into "making a decision for Christ." Give them something appropriate to read, leave them with a prayer, talk to them later—as the Lord gives opportunity.
> —Bill Bright

► **Be honest.**

God does not call us to be spiritual Wikipedias. If we do not know the answers to questions asked, we should say so and offer to research the topic. Our honesty is as important as an excellent answer and reveals that we are still learners.

► **Respect their perspective.**

We should not discount the beliefs or experiences of others. Becoming dismissive is not appropriate or respectful. This does not mean we agree with them; however, we do respect their point of view. This is especially true when discussing beliefs with people of other faiths. Showing curiosity and responding with respect invites reciprocity.

A powerful way to encourage people to reevaluate their beliefs is to ask how their system is working for them. Are they confident about the answers to life's big questions? Is their philosophy of life bringing them joy and satisfaction? Until they sense a need or feel their current worldview is not helping them navigate life, they will probably not consider something new.

▶ **Respond with a faith story.**

Personal stories that paint pictures of how we struggled with similar objections can be powerful. Stories can also build our credibility with nonbelievers as they see how our faith plays out in real life.

BE PREPARED

"Be prepared" is the Boy Scout motto, and it applies to followers of Jesus as well. We need not hold advanced degrees in theology or be skilled apologists, but we do need to be prepared to explain what we believe and why we believe it.

Common Questions

Consider how you would answer if coworkers posed the following objections:

▶ "Christians say God is all-powerful and all-good. If that's so, why doesn't He stop terrorist attacks and sex trafficking and all the suffering in the world?"

▶ "Christians are so condemning and intolerant. I know a lot of people who aren't religious at all, and they seem to be more kind and even more ethical than many Christians. What's up with that?"

▶ "From what I understand, the Bible and the church dictate what Christians should believe and do. I think people should be free to choose how they want to live and be who they want to be. How can you live a truly authentic life otherwise?"

Objections such as these are common. Being prepared with a brief answer not only helps people see the truth, it shows that we have thought about our faith, not just blindly believed something because of how we were raised.

> I came to Christ through apologetics ... I have found that if I am able to speak pragmatically about people's needs and desires and I can back them up with facts, then they listen.
>
> —Norm Miller, Chairman, Interstate Batteries

Common Assumptions That Kill Belief

Behind many objections to the Christian faith are widely accepted assumptions that generate uncertainty and predispose people to think Christianity could not be true. These assumptions, which many in our culture consider commonsense fact, are, in reality, an alternative belief system. Philosophers call them *defeater beliefs*—opinions about something that make it impossible to believe something else.

In *The Reason for God* (Dutton), Tim Keller examines seven common objections to Christianity and identifies the alternative belief system that underlies them. These objections include:

- There cannot be just one true religion.

- A good God would not allow evil and suffering.

- Christianity is a straitjacket.

- The church is responsible for so much injustice.

- A loving God would not send people to hell.

- Science has disproved Christianity.

- The Bible cannot be taken literally.

Keller suggests that in every doubt, faith—not fact—is hidden in the reasoning.[3] And although we may not want to master apologetics or publically debate aggressive atheists, Keller suggests ways we can help people rethink their opinions by causing doubt about their alternative belief system. We can graciously remind them that they are betting their life on something they cannot prove.

Unprovable Assertion	Possible Response
There cannot be just one true religion.	You're betting your life on the belief that a god exists who does not care about how we get to him and that we can make our own rules and shape who god is.
A good God would not allow evil and suffering.	You're betting your life on the belief that a god exists who thinks exactly like you do and is not great enough to have another reason for allowing evil and suffering that you can't understand.
Christianity is a straitjacket.	You're betting your life on the belief that real freedom has no boundaries.
The church is responsible for so much injustice.	You're betting your life on the belief that the actions of a few bad actors nullify the validity of the Christian faith.
A loving God would not send people to hell.	You're betting your life on the belief that a god exists who doesn't hold men and women accountable for their actions.
Science has disproved Christianity.	You're betting your life on the belief that science can empirically disprove God.
The Bible cannot be taken literally.	You're betting your life on the belief that the Bible is unreliable, something that a lot of intelligent people would dispute.

Other good books that provide help to answer tough questions and objections include *I'm Glad You Asked* by Ken Boa and Larry Moody (David C. Cook) and *The Case for Faith* by Lee Strobel (Zondervan).

A number of websites offer helpful resources for both Christians and seeking nonbelievers. They include:

▶ **Reasons to Believe** *(Reasons.org)*

▶ **Probe Ministries** *(Probe.org)*

▶ **The Denison Forum on Truth and Culture**
(DenisonForum.org)

Our Strongest Argument

The strongest evidence for the Christian faith is not a watertight argument, but a watertight person against whom, in the end, there can be no argument.[4] Although we are more sinful than we dare imagine, in Christ we can experience more love than we ever dare dream. Jesus' death as our substitute and what He has done in our lives are the most compelling arguments we have and the ultimate appeal of the Christian faith.

OUR STRONGEST RESOURCE

Jesus promised His supernatural resources to all who join Him in helping to fulfill the Great Commission. He told His disciples,

> All authority in heaven and on earth has been given to me. Therefore go and make disciples of all nations, baptizing them in the name of the Father and of the Son and of the Holy Spirit, and teaching them to obey everything I have commanded you. And surely I am with you always, to the very end of the age. (Matt. 28:18-20)

We are assured of this power and presence today when we join God in drawing people into a relationship with Him.

The Bottom Line

Turn objections into opportunities by answering with grace and humility.

Harvesting

Devote yourselves to prayer, being watchful and thankful.
And pray for us, too, that God may open a door for our message,
so that we may proclaim the mystery of Christ, for which I am in
chains. Pray that I may proclaim it clearly, as I should.
— Colossians 4:2-4

Chapter 12

Making the
Mission Possible

Talking to men for God is a great thing,
but talking to God for men is greater still.
—E. M. Bounds

We are players in The Greatest Story Ever Told. Act I begins with the wonder and beauty of creation, then moves to Adam and Eve's rebellion against God, which brought disharmony and death to them, their race, and the planet on which we live. Fortunately, that is not the end of the story.

The Bible tells us that in God's unchanging commitment to humankind, He had already planned our rescue. Two thousand years ago in the land of ancient Israel, God Himself invaded planet earth. God the Father sent God the Son, empowered by God the Spirit, to pay the penalty for our sins, rescue us from Satan's dominion, give us eternal life, and remake us into the men and women He created us to be.

Through Christ's death, resurrection and ascension, we are set free and made citizens of God's kingdom. Fellowship with our Father has been restored. However, Creation continues to groan under the power of the prince of this world—but not forever. Even now the kingdom of God erupts into our world.

155

The end of the story has been written. The rightful King will return to earth to dwell among men and restore His dominion over our planet. The final mending of the great rupture between God and man will bring healing to all fractured relationships: between men and women, between humanity, and between humanity and the creation.[1]

OUR PLACE IN THE STORY

> Enemy-occupied territory—that is what this world is. Christianity is the story of how the rightful king has landed, you might say landed in disguise, and is calling us all to take part in a great campaign of sabotage.
>
> —C.S. Lewis

Born in the midst of this war between good and evil, we have been called by God to join Him in the cosmic conflict. He does not need us to carry out His plans, yet He gives us this great privilege. He has invited us to join Him in redeeming Creation and participating with the Holy Spirit in drawing people to Himself. *Participating* is a keyword because, as participants, we do not control the outcome.

A farmer cultivates the ground, plants a seed by faith that it will grow. But after the farmer does his work, he cannot force new life to spring from the seed. Neither can we force anyone into new life in Christ. Only God gives life.

> I planted the seed in your hearts, and Apollos watered it, but it was God who made it grow.
>
> —1 Corinthians 3:6 (NLT)

In His infinite wisdom, God ordained that His sovereignty and human responsibility would work together to achieve His purposes. Too grand for our finite minds to comprehend, God calls us to believe this in faith and fulfill our role in His story by seeking to make disciples: cultivating heart soil, planting seeds of truth, and sometimes sharing the privilege of bringing in the harvest and nurturing new life.

THE CHALLENGE

The simplest part of our role in spreading the gospel is also the hardest: prayer. Every phase of the evangelism process—from cultivating to harvesting—depends on prayer. So why is it so hard to pray? Among many reasons, three stand out.

1. Bias for Action

American culture prizes action, accomplishment, efficiency, and productivity. When we slow down to pray, we feel as if we are not accomplishing anything. Without immediate and tangible effect, we perceive we are wasting time. We want to *do something!* C. S. Lewis said the challenge of the Christian life repeats every morning when we wake up and all of our wishes and hopes for the day rush at us like wild animals.

2. Misplaced Confidence

Although we might not admit this aloud, deep down we believe we do not need to pray. Our strong work ethic and the "If you can dream it, you can do it" mindset have helped make America the greatest country on earth. But this mentality has a dark side when it comes to serving God.

In *Living Proof* (NavPress), Jim Peterson reminds us,

> Probably the most dangerous thing about methods is that when they work, we begin to rely on them. We experiment with something. It works. We do it again, and again it works. As we become successful, we slip into thinking that continued success is a matter of just keeping that activity going.[2]

Armed with a good strategy and compelling facts, we feel strong, competent, equal to the task—and forget Jesus' warning, "without Me you can do nothing" (John 15:5).

Walt's Experience

Dave and I hit it off during a business negotiation. Over time, Barb and I became close friends with Dave and his wife, Ann. We spent time together carpooling kids and watching soccer games. Barb and Ann led our daughters' scout troop.

Dave and Ann were not believers, and they had encountered more than a few aggressive, hypocritical Christians, which made Dave wary. But the more we got to know each other, the more my faith seemed to intrigue him.

After a year, over lunch I told Dave how I came to believe in Christ. He listened with interest and asked questions. Eventually, he and Ann accepted an invitation to attend a Bible study at our home. Ann told Barb that she was interested in a personal relationship with Jesus, but she didn't want to take this step without Dave.

For months, I communicated the gospel to Dave in every way I knew. Yet in spite of all my efforts, Dave's heart seemed impenetrable, and I became discouraged.

I met with my spiritual mentor and recounted my frustration. In response, he asked me two tough questions.

"Walt, do you really care about these people, or are they just a project?"

Embarrassed, I had to admit that persuading them to make a decision to trust Jesus had become more important than being a friend.

"How often do you and Barb pray for Dave and Ann?"

I hung my head. "I really don't pray for them very much at all."

He reminded me that Dave and Ann faced the toughest, most important decision of their lives—and that praying for them would do more than all our efforts. So Barb and I began to pray every day for Dave and Ann as we continued to cultivate, plant, and love them.

Almost seven years after our friendship began, God answered our prayers. Dave and Ann both decided to become followers of Jesus.

3. Spiritual Warfare

Evangelism is ultimately about participating in God's plan to reclaim men and women trapped under Satan's control. Paul described our hopeless captivity apart from Christ.

As for you, you were dead in your transgressions and sins, in which you used to live when you followed the ways of this world and of the ruler of the kingdom of the air, the spirit who is now at work in those who are disobedient. All of us also lived among them at one time, gratifying the cravings of our sinful nature and following its desires and thoughts. Like the rest, we were by nature objects of wrath. (Eph. 2:1-3)

Satan knows prayer is the most powerful weapon in our arsenal for freeing men and women from his hold.

SOIL ANALYSIS

Volitional barriers to faith can be the toughest heart-soil challenge to overcome. Even if we gain the intellectual high ground by showing how objections to Christianity do not hold up, this is irrelevant if people do not *want* to believe.

> The concern of the devil is to keep the saints from praying. He fears nothing from prayerless studies, prayerless work, prayerless religion. He laughs at our toil, he mocks at our wisdom, but he trembles when we pray.
>
> —Samuel Chadwick

> People do not believe lies because they have to, but because they want to.
>
> —Malcolm Muggeridge

The struggle to believe is expressed by Arthur Krystal in an article entitled "Why Smart People Believe in God" in Phi Beta Kappa's *American Scholar* journal:

It's easy enough to understand why people want to believe, but actually to believe with one's whole heart and mind in divine grace—that to me is a true miracle.

What's agitating me is religion envy, an unjustifiable resentment of intelligent and skeptical people—I almost said "people who ought to know better"—who swim effortlessly toward the sanctity of dry land, while others, like myself, spiritually adrift, seem unable to strike out for shore. I don't mind admitting that I'm flummoxed by their groundedness, their conviction, their serenity...[3]

Even though Krystal admits his envy of Christian peace and the undeniable pull of the love of a God willing to die for our sins, he cannot bring himself to believe.

> Still, you have to allow others the right of refusal; some can't or won't inhale transcendence. The biblical god is out of the question, not because of intellectual scruples but because of a temperamental predilection to go it alone.[4]

Kystal's experience highlights an important truth: The human will, apart from God's intervention, is unable to respond to Jesus.

> No one can come to me unless the Father who sent me draws him.
> —John 6:44

The volitional barrier is characterized by an unwillingness to consider Christ, regardless of facts or feelings. In their spiritually dead condition, people are predisposed to resist examining spiritual issues or to reject Jesus outright. It is the response of a sinful, fallen nature.

Just as objects are bound to the earth by the force of gravity, without Christ, our will is bound to the world by the force of sin. Human volition has no power to escape the pull of the world or correct the rebellious nature of the soul. Thankfully, God in His love did not to leave us there.

> But because of his great love for us, God, who is rich in mercy, made us alive with Christ even when we were dead in transgressions—it is by grace you have been saved.
> —Ephesians 2:4-5

Apart from the redemptive power of Jesus, worldly values and lifestyles trap every man and woman. Blinded by sin and driven by nagging emptiness, humanity tries everything imaginable to fill the vacuum. When empty people develop life strategies that provide even a meager amount of satisfaction, they find it difficult to look beyond the world to the only One who can fill their hearts. C. S. Lewis likens this struggle to convincing children from the slums to go on a beach vacation when they have never seen the shore:

> We are half-hearted creatures, fooling about with drink and sex and ambition when infinite joy is offered to us, like an ignorant child who wants to go on making mud pies in a slum because he cannot imagine what is meant by the offer of a holiday at the sea. We are far too easily pleased.[5]

When we encounter someone with a volitional barrier, we must remember this central truth: Evangelism begins and ends with God. He has invited us to partner with Him in the privileged mission of redeeming souls. We do our part in cultivating, planting, praying for the harvest, and seeking His guidance. The rest is in His hands.

Harvesting Phase in a Nutshell

Possible Steps of Faith	HARVESTING
Considers the truth of the gospel	Speaks to the Will
▼	**The Obstacles**
Recognizes personal need of God	Volitional Barriers: Cultural Pressure, Indecision, Rejection, Spiritual Deadness
▼	
Sees Jesus as the answer	**Key Activities**
▼	Continued Encouragement and Prayer
Turns from self-trust	**The Goal**
▼	
Trusts in Christ	Trust in Jesus

FIRST CENTURY STRATEGY FOR SUCCESS

The rapid and far-reaching spread of the gospel in the first century was due to the mass mobilization of ordinary Christians and the persistent pattern of prayer of the early church. The vital role of prayer is recorded throughout the book of Acts.

- ► As the early church waited for the promised Holy Spirit to bestow power to be Jesus' witnesses, "They all joined together constantly in prayer..." (Acts 1:14).

- ► The apostles prayed for guidance as they sought a new colleague to replace Judas: "Then they prayed, 'Lord, you know everyone's heart. Show us which of these two you have chosen'" (Acts 1:24).

- ► After Pentecost, prayer was a key activity of Jesus' followers in Jerusalem: "They devoted themselves to the apostles' teaching and to the fellowship, to the breaking of bread and to prayer" (Acts 2:42).

- ► Their devotion to prayer brought forth revival in Jerusalem: "And the Lord added to their number daily those who were being saved" (Acts 2:47).

- ► When Peter and John were released after their first arrest, the church prayed: "When they heard this, they raised their voices together in prayer to God. ... And they were all filled with the Holy Spirit and spoke the word of God boldly" (Acts 4:24, 31).

- ► As the church moved beyond Jerusalem, prayer was key to the joy and freedom the gospel brought to Samaria: "When they arrived, they prayed for them that they might receive the Holy Spirit" (Acts 8:15).

As the narrative in Acts continues, focused on Paul's efforts to spread the gospel, we find the same emphasis on prayer.

► Paul prayed immediately after his dramatic conversion on the road to Damascus (Acts 9:11).

► Prayer was the pattern of the disciples' ministry (Acts 9:40; 10:9).

► The gospel came to the first Gentile believers—the Roman centurion Cornelius and his family—in response to prayer (Acts 10:30–31).

► When Peter was thrown into prison for preaching the gospel, the church prayed and witnessed his miraculous release (Acts 12:5).

► Before the church at Antioch sent Paul and Barnabas out to spread the gospel through what is now Turkey, they prayed (Acts 13:3).

► Before Paul and Barnabas took leave of the new believers in a town where they had ministered, they prayed (Acts 14:23).

► When Paul and Silas were thrown into prison for proclaiming Jesus, they prayed (Acts 16:25).

► Before Paul left the followers of Jesus in Ephesus and Tyre, he spent time with them in prayer (Acts 20:36; 21:5).

► Paul prayed for his captors to come to believe in Jesus (Acts 26:29).

► The last miracle in the book of Acts was empowered by prayer (Acts 28:8).

Today, with technology and strategies of every stripe at our disposal, it is easy to become obsessed with tools and techniques. But they are just that, tools and techniques. They are useless if not empowered by the Spirit through prayer.

In many ways, our advantages exceed those of the early church, but in reality we have no more power than they did. And we have less if we fail to pray.

> Men may spurn our appeals, reject our message, oppose our arguments, despise our persons, but they are helpless against our prayers.
>
> —J. Sidlow Baxter

PRAYING FOR OURSELVES

We cannot accomplish anything of spiritual significance unless the Spirit is working within us. Following are examples of how we can pray for ourselves as Christ's ambassadors in the workplace. We can ask that...

- ▶ we will do excellent work that attracts others' attention (Prov. 22:29).

- ▶ our work will bring glory to God (Matt. 5:16).

- ▶ we will treat people fairly (Col. 4:1).

- ▶ we will have a good reputation with unbelievers (1 Thess. 4:12).

- ▶ others will see Jesus in us (Phil. 2:12–16).

- ▶ our lives will make our faith attractive (Titus 2:10).

- ▶ our conversations will be wise, sensitive, grace-filled, and enticing (Col. 4:5–6).

- ▶ we will be bold and fearless (Eph. 6:19).

- ▶ we will be alert to open doors (Col. 4:3).

- ▶ we will be able to clearly explain the gospel (Col. 4:4).

- ▶ God will expand our influence (1 Chron. 4:10).

PRAYING FOR OTHERS

We can pray for coworkers and friends, asking that...

- ▶ the Father will draw them to Himself (John 6:44).

- ▶ they will seek to know God (Deut. 4:29; Acts 17:27).

- ▶ they will believe the Bible (Rom. 10:17; 1 Thess. 2:13).

- ▶ Satan will be restrained from blinding them from the truth (Matt. 13:19; 2 Cor. 4:4).

- ▶ the Holy Spirit will convict them of sin, righteousness, and judgment (John 16:8–13).

- ▶ God will send other Christians into their lives to influence them toward Jesus (Matt. 9:37–38).

- ▶ they will believe in Jesus as their Savior (John 1:12; 5:24).

- ▶ they will turn from sin (Acts 3:19; 17:30–31).

- ▶ they will confess Jesus as Lord (Rom. 10:9–10).

- ▶ they will yield their lives and follow Jesus (Mark 8:34–37; Rom. 12:1–2; 2 Cor. 5:15; Phil. 3:7–8).

- ▶ they will grow in Jesus (Col. 2:6–7).

- ▶ they will become a positive influence for Jesus in their arena of influence (2 Tim. 2:2).

Prayer is what moves the Hand that moves the human heart to faith and makes our mission possible.

Bottom Line

Evangelism depends on prayer more than anything else.

Multiplying

Therefore go and make disciples of all nations,
baptizing them in the name of the Father and of the Son
and of the Holy Spirit, and teaching them
to obey everything I have commanded you."
— Matthew 28:19-20

Chapter 13

Launching New Believers

He gave His life for you, so He could give His life to you,
so He could live His life through you.
—Major Ian Thomas

I
n the Great Commission, Jesus did not mandate that we sign up new recruits or volunteers for His kingdom agenda. He told us to make disciples.

The word disciple occurs 269 times in the New Testament. Christian is found three times and was first introduced to refer precisely to the disciples—in a situation where it was no longer possible to regard them as a sect of the Jews. The New Testament is a book about disciples, by disciples, and for disciples of Jesus Christ.[1]

Being used by God to guide others to place their trust in Christ and receive His free gift of salvation is a great privilege. But the job is not finished. No matter how old we are biologically, we are born into the family of God as infants in Christ.[2] A fundamental need of any infant is proper nourishment and training to promote healthy growth.

> Like newborn babies, crave pure spiritual milk, so that by it you may grow up in your salvation, now that you have tasted that the Lord is good.
> —1 Peter 2:2-3

When God uses us in the birthing process of new disciples, this does not mean we become like spiritual family physicians, providing total care. It does mean that we should help them begin their new life in Christ and find other believers to come alongside to help with spiritual development.

THE LAUNCH PROCESS

Paul explained to Christians in Ephesus that each person in the body of Christ has a role to play in helping others come to Jesus and then grow in their relationship with Him.

> From him the whole body, joined and held together by every supporting ligament, grows and builds itself up in love, as each part does its work.
> —Ephesians 4:16

Paul had experienced the work of the body of Christ firsthand after his dramatic conversion on the road to Damascus. To help launch Paul into his new life as a disciple, Jesus sent Ananias,[3] who did four things:

He took the initiative. We need to initiate times of regular contact with new converts to help them acclimate to their new life in Christ. They need to know they do not have to figure things out on their own.

He prayed. New disciples often have questions about how to pray and what to pray for. Many have never prayed aloud with another person. We can pray that God will unleash the power of the Holy Spirit in new disciples, and encourage them to be alert for how God is at work in their lives every day.

He facilitated Paul's baptism. Immediately after Paul received his sight, he was baptized. Baptism is a step of obedience and how we identify ourselves as followers of Jesus. Baptism can also help deepen the understanding of new believers about what it means to be a disciple of Jesus.

He met practical and spiritual needs. Ananias brought Paul food and introduced him to other disciples in Damascus. We can help new disciples with practical aspects of their new life, such as choosing a good study Bible, introducing them to other believers, and helping them get involved in a church.

ELEMENTS OF GROWTH

In the book of Acts, Luke records the activities of the early church and gives numerous examples of the cornerstone role of Christian community. Being part of a local, like-minded community of believers is vital to every disciple's growth.

► Community provides a setting where believers regularly remind each other of God's love and commitment, and the hope we have in Christ.

► Community is a place of refuge and refreshment. We benefit and grow by giving and receiving affirmation and encouragement from believers of all ages. This is especially true for new believers.

► Community has physical benefits as well. Medical studies reveal that the social support provided by a loving community increases the quality and length of life.[4] Dozens of other studies indicate that healthy relationships matter and loneliness can kill.

Fifty days after Christ's ascension, three thousand men and women became new disciples in response to the miracle of Pentecost and Peter's preaching of the gospel.[5] In response to this flood of new converts, Luke describes four practices of the early church that contributed to their spiritual development and spread of the gospel. These practices are just as relevant today.

> They devoted themselves to the apostles' teaching and to the fellowship, to the breaking of bread and to prayer. Everyone was filled with awe, and many wonders and miraculous signs were done by the apostles. All the believers were together and had everything in common. Selling their possessions and goods, they gave to anyone as

> he had need. Every day they continued to meet together in the temple courts. They broke bread in their homes and ate together with glad and sincere hearts, praising God and enjoying the favor of all the people. And the Lord added to their number daily those who were being saved.
>
> —Acts 2:42-47

1. Learning

The new disciples "devoted themselves to the apostles' teaching," intentionally learning more about God and His Word. Learning to read and study the Bible, both personally and with other believers, is essential to the spiritual growth of new believers.

Consider the importance of God's word:

▶ It contains the truth and sets us free. (John 8:31–32)

▶ It is alive and penetrates the heart. (Heb. 4:12)

▶ It shows us the truth, exposes our rebellion, corrects our mistakes, trains us to live God's way, equips us for good work. (2 Tim. 3:16-17)

▶ It helps us to face temptation. (Psalm 119:9, 11)

▶ It guides our path. (Psalm 119:105)

▶ It makes us wise. (Psalm 19:7)

2. Serving

The new disciples "devoted themselves to fellowship." Fellowship is about sharing and serving to meet the spiritual, physical, and emotional needs of others in the body of Christ.

Being attentive to the needs of others is countercultural in our me-centered world. But this is what Jesus modeled, and He calls and empowers us to do the same.

> Whoever wants to be first must be slave of all. For even the Son of Man did not come to be served, but to serve, and to give his life as a ransom for many.
>
> —Mark 10:44-45

We need not look far for opportunities to help others. It starts in our own work. Seeing our daily work as an opportunity to meet legitimate needs is vital to spiritual growth and serves as a witness of our faith in Christ.[6] Guiding new believers to understand this truth is an important step in discipleship.

> Nothing disciplines the inordinate desires of the flesh like service, and nothing transforms the desires of the flesh like serving in hiddenness. The flesh whines against service, but it screams against hidden service. It strains and pulls for honor and recognition.
>
> —Richard Foster

3. Evangelism

When we become part of God's family, we join Christian brothers and sisters around the world in fulfilling the Great Commission. The new life God implants in us is meant to penetrate and be multiplied in the lives of others.

Although new followers of Christ have much to learn, they can still be powerful witnesses. Consider the Samaritan woman, who immediately told others about her encounter with Jesus, and many Samaritans believed.[7] The blind man healed by Jesus testified in a simple but compelling manner about what had happened to him.[8] He did not understand theology, but he knew what he had experienced. God also used new disciples in the early church to spread the gospel.[9]

4. Worship

Luke tells us that the new believers joined the early church in worship. Worship is a contraction of two words—worth and ship, so to worship is to ascribe worth. Worship is recognizing and responding appropriately to who God is—at church, at home, at work, and in every area of life.

> If you cannot worship the Lord in the midst of your responsibilities on Monday, it is not very likely that you were worshiping on Sunday.
> —A.W. Tozer

To new believers, it may be surprising to learn that the body of Christ worships God in many ways: We worship when we sing, pray, and celebrate His mercy and love in the context of community. We worship Him when we stand in awe of His mighty power and contemplate the beauty and wonder of creation. We also worship Him by obeying His Word. For example, we are worshipping when we love and respect our spouse and children or refuse to take advantage of a situation at work because we know that the choice would not honor God.

> And whatever you do, whether in word or deed, do it all in the name of the Lord Jesus, giving thanks to God the Father through him.
> —Colossians 3:17

THE GROWTH PROCESS

Launching new disciples requires more than guiding them to a spiritual community that provides growth opportunities. We should help them understand the growth process itself.

Many exciting changes lie in store for new disciples. As we mentor them, we should explain what happens the moment any of us embrace Christ as Savior. An amazing transformation began to take place. We became new creatures in Christ, sharing in His resurrection life.[10]

> There is nothing more important to learn about Christian growth than this: Growing in grace means becoming like Christ.
> —Sinclair B. Ferguson

The moment of our rebirth, the Holy Spirit puts God's plan into effect to transform us into the likeness of Christ.[11] He becomes our tutor, teaching us God's will. He changes us from the inside out as the He reorients our mind, will, and emotions to the reality of our new life.

New believers need to understand that transformation is not something that the Holy Spirit does alone. In Colossians 3, Paul explains that we have a part in the process as well.

> Since, then, you have been raised with Christ, set your hearts on things above, where Christ is seated at the right hand of God. Set your minds on things above, not on earthly things. For you died, and your life is now hidden with Christ in God. When Christ, who is your life, appears, then you also will appear with him in glory
> —Colossians 3:1-4

New Thoughts

Spiritual growth begins when we intentionally focus our minds on the spiritual realities of our new identity in Christ, and reckon them true. Although new believers may look the same in the mirror, it is vital that we help them to understand that a great exchange has taken place. Like us...

- ► they were guilty; now they are forgiven.

- ► they were alienated; now they are accepted by God.

- ► they were in bondage; now they are set free.

- ► they were rebels; now they are sons and daughters of the King.

- ► they were victims; now they are victors.

- ► they were impotent to change; now they are able to become all that God created them to be.

As new believers personalize these facts and begin to understand more fully how their old life died and has been replaced with Christ's life, they will begin to change from the inside out.

New Choices

Satan delights in tempting believers—new and old. He is particularly adept at encouraging believers to meet personal needs in ways God did not intend, which can lead to bad habits, and even strongholds and addictions. Paul calls these behaviors idolatry because we look to them rather than God to meet our deepest longings.

However, because of our new life in Christ, we have the ability to choose to act in ways that reflect this reality. Explaining this power to new believers and serving as living examples of how God empowers us to make good decisions is included in our role as spiritual mentors.

Paul warns that many attitudes and actions need to be *put to death* because they do not belong to a new life in Christ. And, by faith, we replace these with choices that reflect this new identity.

> Put to death, therefore, whatever belongs to your earthly nature: sexual immorality, impurity, lust, evil desires and greed, which is idolatry. Because of these, the wrath of God is coming. You used to walk in these ways, in the life you once lived. But now you must rid yourselves of all such things as these: anger, rage, malice, slander, and filthy language from your lips.
>
> Do not lie to each other, since you have taken off your old self with its practices and have put on the new self, which is being renewed in knowledge in the image of its Creator.
>
> Here there is no Greek or Jew, circumcised or uncircumcised, barbarian, Scythian, slave or free, but Christ is all, and is in all. Therefore, as God's chosen people, holy and dearly loved, clothe yourselves with compassion, kindness, humility, gentleness and patience. Bear with each other and forgive whatever grievances you may have against one another. Forgive as the Lord forgave you. And over all these virtues put on love, which binds them all together in perfect unity.
>
> —Colossians 3:5–14

Paul is not unrealistic about how hard it is to jettison old lifestyle choices, and we should acknowledge this to new believers. The emotional stress is intense. Satan has trained our hearts to believe that we cannot survive without attitudes and activities we used in the past to sustain our old way of life.

New Emotions

Paul warns us about this rebellion of our emotions and explains how to confront them with the truth. New believers need our guidance and our knowledge of Scripture to battle the emotional challenges they will face as followers of Christ

> Let the peace of Christ rule in your hearts, since as members of one body you were called to peace. And be thankful. Let the word of Christ dwell in you richly as you teach and admonish one another with all wisdom, and as you sing psalms, hymns and spiritual songs with gratitude in your hearts to God.
>
> —Colossians 3:15-16

The words Paul uses are graphic. Peace is not just peace of mind, but wholeness—spiritual health, prosperity, and position in Christ. The Greek word, *brabeuō*, translated *rule*, means to act as an umpire. Paul is saying, *Don't let anyone, anything, or any circumstance call you out when Christ calls you safe.* New believers need to hear this truth spoken again and again so that it sinks deeply into their souls. As new believers soak up God's Word, personally and in community, they can give thanks for the truth that their deepest longings are met in Christ— even when their emotions cry for what will never satisfy.

THE ROAD AHEAD

If the process of evangelism is a long process, the growth process is longer still. New Christians will not always make

> The Christian does not think God will love us because we are good, but that God will make us good because He loves us.
>
> —C.S. Lewis

wise choices. As we seek to help them enter the growth process, we need patience—and we need others.

Life change is the Holy Spirit's job. It is the Holy Spirit at work in the heart of every believer that transforms the mind, will, and emotions to reflect Christ.

However, just as He does in evangelism, God uses others in the body of Christ to help in the process of discipleship. New Christians need pastors and teachers to instruct them. They may need counselors to help them break free from old thought processes and patterns of behavior. But most of all they need brothers and sister to walk with them and encourage them along the way. And they need all of us to love and pray for them as they step into the beauty of their new life in Christ.

The Bottom Line

Salvation is just the beginning of eternal life.

One Life at a Time

One's task is not to turn the world upside down,
but to do what is necessary at the given place
and with a due consideration of reality.
—Dietrich Bonhoeffer

I n his 2014 commencement address to eight thousand University
of Texas graduates, Admiral William H. McRaven, ninth
commander of U.S. Special Operations Command, said average
Americans will meet ten thousand people in their lifetime.

"…if every one of you changed the lives of just 10 people, and
each one of those folks changed the lives of another 10 people—
just 10—then in five generations, 125 years, the class of 2014 will
have changed the lives of 800 million people. ...

"…changing the world can happen anywhere and anyone can do it."

McRaven described how he witnessed one person make a difference
every day he served in the Middle East. For example, a young army
officer decided to go left instead of right down a road in Baghdad,
saving ten soldiers and himself from an ambush. In Afghanistan,

another officer sensed something was not quite right, so she directed a platoon away from an area—and avoided a five-hundred-pound IED, saving the soldiers' lives, as well as their children yet unborn, and their children's children.

> Take the first step in faith. You don't have to see the whole staircase, just take the first step.
>
> —Martin Luther King

In his book, *Things That Matter* (Crown Publishing), Charles Krauthammer remarks that the world today would be unrecognizable—dark, impoverished, tortured—had totalitarianism won in the twentieth century. Its demise turned on one man.

"... victory required one man without whom the fight would have been lost at the beginning. It required Winston Churchill."[2]

GOD WORKS ONE ON ONE

Since the beginning of time, God has used individuals to carry out His plans and purposes. It is not governments, societies, institutions, corporations, families, or even churches that change the world, but the individuals within those entities.

God has never looked for people of great intellect or great giftedness to do His bidding. He looks for people who are willing to follow Him and practice His presence in every arena of life.

> For the eyes of the LORD range throughout the earth to strengthen those whose hearts are fully committed to him.
>
> —2 Chronicles 16:9

One man committed to doing this and made a significant difference in Great Britain. William Wilberforce was born in the mid-1700s. At age twenty-one, he was elected to parliament. When he came to faith in Jesus in his mid-twenties, Wilberforce considered leaving his government post to pursue theological studies.

John Newton, a pastor and former slave trader, encouraged Wilberforce to remain in public service, believing God had a purpose for him there. On October 28, 1787, Wilberforce wrote in his diary, "God has set before me two objects, the suppression of the Slave Trade and the reformation of manners."[3] His vision was audacious, for abolishing the slave trade would require closing down an economic enterprise that contributed millions of pounds sterling to the British economy. And reforming manners would mean transforming Britain's decadent culture.

> How wonderful that no one need wait a single moment to improve the world.
>
> —Anne Frank

Three days before Wilberforce died on July 26, 1833, the bill for the abolition of slavery passed its second reading in the House of Commons. And by the end of the century, Christian virtues had become fashionable, overshadowing the loose morality and corrupt public life that previously defined his country.

Rarely has the power of one individual been so poignantly demonstrated. But a closer look at Wilberforce's life reveals that he did not work alone. A network of Christian friends joined their energy with his. Together, these men and women operated like "a meeting which never adjourned,"[4] as they pursued godly change in their society. One person can change the world but never alone.

OUR MISSION

Because first-century Christians took the Great Commission seriously and took their faith into the workplace, the Good News spread throughout the Mediterranean region—and continued to spread from continent to continent, century after century. We are the beneficiaries of their faithfulness.

Today, God calls us to do the same—to play our role in the Great Commission and take our faith to work. The preceding chapters explained thirteen bottom-line principles for our mission.

▶ Evangelism is a process, not an event. God has gifted each of us to play a critical role in drawing people to Himself. Our job is to discover where the Holy Spirit is working in a person's life and join Him there.

▶ You do not have to leave the workplace to know the joy of being used by God. He can use you right where you are.

▶ As Christians, we have what people want. We simply need to communicate in winsome ways they can understand.

▶ Christ calls all believers to be His witnesses. But our lives always come before our lips.

▶ In God's plan to take the gospel to the human race, small things add up to big things that make a big difference.

▶ Stories can resonate with the listener's longings and evoke consideration of gospel truth on an emotional level.

▶ Evangelism is a team activity. Network with others for maximum spiritual impact.

> The Great Commission is not an option to be considered; it is a command to be obeyed.
> —Hudson Taylor

▶ Jesus calls us the salt of the earth. For salt to make a difference, it has to make contact.

▶ When a door opens for planting seeds of truth, walk through wisely. If it closes, don't try to open a window. Wait on God's timing. He is at work.

▶ To be effective ambassadors for Christ, we should learn to communicate the gospel in a clear, concise way that connects to the felt needs of the listener.

▶ Turn objections into opportunities by responding with grace and humility.

▶ Evangelism depends on prayer more than anything else.

▶ Salvation is just the beginning of eternal life.

Jesus began his earthly ministry with evangelism by calling four fishermen to become fishers of men.[5] He ended His earthly ministry by appointing His disciples to be His witnesses throughout the world.[6] None of us is equal to the task, but Christ has promised to give us strength and courage to do what He has called us to do.

> I can do all things through Him who strengthens me.
> —Philippians 4:13

May we all hear, "Well done, good and faithful servant," when we enter our Master's presence.

ENDNOTES

Introduction

1. Rodney Stark, *The Rise of Christianity: A Sociologist Reconsiders History,* (Princeton, NJ: Princeton University Press, 1996), Page 6.

2. "Three Trends on Faith, Work and Calling," Barna Group, February 11, 2014, *https://www.barna.org/barna-update/culture/649-three-major-faith-and-culture-trends-for-2014.*

3. Hartford Institute for Religion Research estimates there are roughly 314,000 protestant congregations and other Christian churches, and 24,000 Catholic and Orthodox churches in the United States. This estimate relies on the 2010 RCMS (Religious Congregations Membership Study) religious congregations census. *http://hirr.hartsem.edu/research/fastfacts/fast_facts.html.*

4. *The Yearbook of American and Canadian Churches* reported that there were 600,000 clergy serving in various denominations in the United States, not including clergy serving independent churches, not tied to a denomination. *http://hirr.hartsem.edu/research/fastfacts/fast_facts.html#numclergy.*

5. "'Nones' on the Rise," Pew Research Center, October 9, 2012, *http://www.pewforum.org/2012/10/09/nones-on-the-rise.* Christians in other countries recognize the huge mission field in America. The United States receives more missionaries that any other country according to Center for the Study of Global Christianity at Gordon-Conwell Theological Seminary *http://www.gordonconwell.com/netcommunity/CSGCResources/ChristianityinitsGlobalContext.pdf.*

6. We use the term nonbeliever to describe people who have not placed their faith in Jesus Christ as their Savior, not to indicate no belief at all. Everyone bases their life on some belief whether they think of it as an act of faith or not.

7. *The Saline Solution* was developed in 1995 for the Christian Medical and Dental Associations as a live conference and later was published as a video curriculum. In 2014, this material for healthcare professionals was revised, updated and is now available as both a live conference and video curriculum entitled *Grace Prescriptions.*

8. *Workplace Grace* is also available as a six-week video curriculum. Learn more at *https://www.CenterForFaithAndWork.com/article/workplace-grace-dvd-curriculum.*

Chapter 1: Spiritual Economics

1. According to Eric Holt-Gimenez, executive director of Food First, "The world already produces more than one and one-half times enough food to feed everyone on the planet. That's enough to feed ten billion people." "We Already Grow Enough Food For 10 Billion People and Still Can't End Hunger," Eric Holt-Gimenez, executive director of Food First/Institute for Food and Development Policy, *Huffington Post, May, 2, 2012, http://www.huffingtonpost.com/eric-holt-gimenez/world-hunger_b_1463429.html.*

2. "Three Trends on Faith, Work and Calling," Barna Group, February 11, 2014, *https://www.barna.org/barna-update/culture/649-three-major-faith-and-culture-trends-for-2014.*

3. "Three Major Faith and Culture Trends for 2014," Barna Group, January 21, 2014, *https://www.barna.org/barna-update/culture/652-3-vocational-trends-for-2014*.

4. "Is Evangelism Going Out of Style?," Barna Group, December 18, 2013, *https://www.barna.org/barna-update/faith-spirituality/648-is-evangelism-going-out-of-style*.

5. "Survey Describes the Spiritual Gifts That Christians Say They Have," The Barna Group, February 9, 2009, *https://www.barna.org/barna-update/faith-spirituality/211-survey-describes-the-spiritual-gifts-that-christians-say-they-have*.

6. Jim Engle devised a scale to illustrate the decision-making steps that a person might go through before they reach spiritual maturity. We have taken the liberty to adapt and expand this concept to the four phases of evangelism.

7. Win and Charles Arn, *The Master's Plan for Making Disciples* (Grand Rapids: Baker, 1998), 45–46.

8. Ibid, 48.

Chapter 2: Called to the Workplace

1. James Davison Hunter. *To Change the World: The Irony, Tragedy, & Possibility of Christianity in the Late Modern World*, (New York: Oxford University Press, 2010), p. 227.

2. "Opportunity Knocks," London Institute for Contemporary Christianity, *http://www.licc.org.uk/resources/2010/08/07/opportunity-knocks/*.

3. "Massive 6-to-1 Majority Favors Tougher Regulation of Wall Street," Harris Interactive, May 20, 2011, *http://www.harrisinteractive.com/NewsRoom/HarrisPolls/tabid/447/ctl/ReadCustom%20Default/mid/1508/ArticleId/783/Default.aspx Accessed January 10, 2014*.

4. Quote from the inaugural address given at the dedication of the Free University in Amsterdam. Found in *Abraham Kuyper: A Centennial Reader*, ed. James D. Bratt (Grand Rapids, MI, Eerdmans, 1998), 488.

5. Abraham Kuyper, *Lectures on Calvinism*, (Grand Rapids: Eerdmans, 1931), p. 53.

Chapter 3: Is Anyone Hungry?

1. Jay Conrad Levinson and Shel Horowitz, *Guerrilla Marketing Goes Green* (John Wiley & Sons, Inc.: Hoboken, N.J., 2010), 4.

2. "How the Last Decade Changed American Life," Barna Group, July 31, 2013, *https://www.barna.org/barna-update/culture/624-how-the-last-decade-changed-american-life*.

3. Ibid.

4. "Three Trends on Faith, Work and Calling," Barna Group, February 11, 2014, *https://www.barna.org/barna-update/culture/649-three-major-faith-and-culture-trends-for-2014*.

5. "The State of the Bible Report 2014," American Bible Society, April 9, 2014, *http://www.americanbible.org/features/state-of-the-bible-research-2014*.

6. "What surveys say about worship attendance – and why some stay home," Pew Research Center, September 13, 2013, *http://www.pewresearch.org/fact-*

tank/2013/09/13/what-surveys-say-about-worship-attendance-and-why-some-stay-home.

7. "Americans Divided on the Importance of Church," Barna Group, March 25, 2014, *https://www.barna.org/barna-update/culture/661-americans-divided-on-the-importance-of-church.*

8. "What surveys say about worship attendance – and why some stay home," Pew Research Center, September 13, 2013, *.http://www.pewresearch.org/fact-tank/2013/09/13/what-surveys-say-about-worship-attendance-and-why-some-stay-home.*

9. Ibid.

10. "Americans' Belief in God, Miracles and Heaven Declines," Harris Interactive, December 16, 2013, *http://www.harrisinteractive.com/NewsRoom/HarrisPolls/tabid/447/ctl/ReadCustom%20Default/mid/1508/ArticleId/1353/Default.aspx.*

11. "For many, 'Losing My Religion' isn't just a song: It's life," *USA Today*, January 3, 2012, *http://usatoday30.usatoday.com/news/religion/story/2011-12-25/religion-god-atheism-so-what/52195274/1.*

12. "For many, 'Losing My Religion' isn't just a song: It's life," *USA Today*, January 3, 2012, *http://usatoday30.usatoday.com/news/religion/story/2011-12-25/religion-god-atheism-so-what/52195274/1.*

13. "What surveys say about worship attendance – and why some stay home," Pew Research Center, September 13, 2013, *http://www.pewresearch.org/fact-tank/2013/09/13/what-surveys-say-about-worship-attendance-and-why-some-stay-home.*

14. "New Census Bureau Report Analyzes Nation's Linguistic Diversity," United States Census Bureau, April 27, 2010, *http://www.census.gov/newsroom/releases/archives/american_community_survey_acs/cb10-cn58.html.*

15. "Limited English Proficient Population of the United States," Migration Policy Institute, July 25, 2013, *http://www.migrationpolicy.org/article/limited-english-proficient-population-united-states#20.*

16. "State of the Bible 2013," American Bible Society, *http://www.americanbible.org/state-bible, Accessed March 6, 2014.*

17. Walter L. Larimore and William C. Peel, *The Saline Solution* (Bristol, Tenn.: The Paul Tournier Institute, 1996), 19.

18. "Tolerance," Oxford Dictionaries, *http://www.oxforddictionaries.com/us/definition/american_english/tolerance. Accessed May 6, 2014.*

19. "Deconstructing Defeater Beliefs: Leading the Secular to Christ," essay by Tim Keller, Senior Pastor, Redeemer Presbyterian Church, New York, 2004.

Chapter 4: Earning the Right to Be Heard

1. Elton Trueblood, *The Company of the Committed*, (New York: Harper & Publishers, 1961), 53.

2. John Fischer, *Fearless Faith* (Eugene, Ore.: Harvest House, 2002), 198.

3. "Christians: More Like Jesus or Pharisees?" The Barna Group, April 30, 2013, *https://www.barna.org/barna-update/faith-spirituality/611-christians-more-like-jesus-or-pharisees*.

Chapter 5: Keep It Simple

1. Bekah Wright, "These airlines had the least and most complaints last year", Yahoo Travel, posted February 12, 2014, *http://travel.yahoo.com/blogs/compass/these-airlines-had-the-least-and-most-complaints-last-year-172459025.html*.

2. Tom Peters, *The Circle of Innovation* (New York: Knopf, 1997), 460.

3. Luke 9:54

4. Matthew 14:28-29

5. Mark 10:35-41

6. Exodus 4

7. 1 Samuel 17

8. John 6

9. "77% Think Americans Are Getting Ruder," Rasmussen Reports, October 17, 2013, *http://www.rasmussenreports.com/public_content/lifestyle/general_lifestyle/october_2013/77_think_americans_are_getting_ruder*.

10. "Acts of kindness spread surprisingly easily: just a few people can make a difference," *Science Daily*, March 10, 2010, *http://www.sciencedaily.com/releases/2010/03/100308151049.htm*.

Chapter 6: Fostering Curiosity

1. Leo Widrich, "The Science of Storytelling: Why Telling a Story is the Most Powerful Way to Activate Our Brains," December 5, 2012, *http://lifehacker.com/5965703/the-science-of-storytelling-why-telling-a-story-is-the-most-powerful-way-to-activate-our-brains*.

Chapter 7: Building a Spiritual Network

1. Brigid Schulte, "Why being too busy makes us feel so good," *The Washington Post*, March 14, 2014, *http://www.washingtonpost.com/opinions/why-being-too-busy-makes-us-feel-so-good/2014/03/14/c098f6c8-9e81-11e3-a050-dc3322a94fa7_story.html*.

2. Genesis 1:1-2; 2:7; Job 26:13; Psalm 33:6; Proverbs 8:22-36; John 1:1-3; Ephesians 1:11; Colossians 1:16-17; Mark 10:45; John 1:18; 6:44; 16:8-10; Ephesians 1:3-15; 1 Peter 3:18

3. Genesis 2:18

4. Exodus 36

5. Nehemiah 3

6. Mark 3:14-19

7. Luke 10:1

8. Acts 3:1; 6:5; 9:27; 11:25-26; 13:2; 14:1; 15:39-40; 16:1-3;, 22; 18:1-5, 18

9. Paul Brand, M.D., *The Challenge of Evangelism for the Medical and Dental Professions*, ed. Leonard W. Ritzman, M.D., (Dallas, Tex.: The Christian Medical and Dental Society, n.d.), 21.

10. See Acts 11:20–26; 13:2–5; 15:39–16:5.

11. Colossians 3:22-25

12. Acts 9:26-27

13. Marketplace Chaplains was founded in 1984 by Gil Stricklin. For more information see *http://mchapusa.com*. Corporate Chaplains of American was founded by Mark Cress in 1996. For more information see *http://www.chaplain.org*.

Chapter 8: No Impact Without Contact

1. "Cocooning: It's back and thanks to tech, it's bigger," Faith Popcorn's BrainReserve, February 19, 2013, *http://www.faithpopcorn.com/super-cocooning/*.

2. Ibid.

3. Ibid.

4. Robert D. Putnam, *Bowling Alone: the Collapse and Revival of American Community*, (New York: Simon & Schuster Publishers, 2000), p. 115.

5. Matthew 5:13

6. "Salt," Jewish Encyclopedia, accessed May 6, 2014, *http://www.jewishencyclopedia.com/articles/13043-salt*.

7. Eberhard J. Wormer, "A taste for salt in the history of medicine," *Science Tribune*, March 1999, *http://www.tribunes.com/tribune/sel/worm.htm#b*.

8. Philippians 2:6–8

9. Luke 7:34

10. John 17:13-21

11. Matthew 5:13

12. Acts 26:18

13. 2 Timothy 2:26

14. John 16:8-10

15. Romans 14:3-5

Chapter 9: Walking Through Open Doors

1. John 4:4-26

2. John 3:1-15

3. Acts 26:2-29

Chapter 10: The Whole Truth

1. Karl Gruber, "Common Denominators of Good Ambassadors," *http://www.ediplomat.com/nd/essays/gruber.htm*, accessed June 8, 2014.

2. Adapted from Timothy J. Keller, Center Church, (Grand Rapids: Zondervan, 2012), 114-5.

3. Genesis 3:10

4. Romans 8:1; John 4:18

5. Hebrews 2:14-18; 1 Corinthians 15:55-57

6. Romans 3:23-24

7. Hebrews 9:14; 10:19-22

8. 1 Corinthians 1:18-31; Ephesians 3:9-12.

9. Luke 17:11-13; Mark 2:1-12; Matthew 11:28-29; 1 Corinthians 10:13

10. John 3:16; Romans 8:31-16; 1 John 4:10

11. Compare Genesis 1:28 with Genesis 3:16-24

12. Romans 8:5

13. Philippians 4:3; Ephesians 3:20

14. Acts 17:28; Ephesians 1:11; Revelation 4:11

15. Exodus 34:6

16. Ephesians 1:11-14

17. Philippians 2:6-11

18. John 1:14-18

19. 2 Corinthians 5:21; 1 Peter 3:18

20. John 11:24; Colossians 3:1-4

21. John 1:12; 3:15-16, 36; 6:35-36, 40; 11:25-26; 20:31; 1 John 5:11-13

22. John 3:16; 1 John 2:1-2; 5:11-13

23. Romans 8:31-39

24. 1 Corinthians 10:31; Colossians 3:1-16

25. Other passages include 2 Corinthians 5:21; Romans 5:8; 1 Peter 3:18; Psalm 103:12.

26. Chuck Swindoll, *Growing Strong in the Seasons of Life* (Grand Rapids: Zondervan, 1994) p. 61.

27. Luke 15:7, 10

Chapter 11: Facing Objections

1. Ephesians 4:19

2. This list of responses, as well as the preceding list, was adapted from "Heart for the Harvest" seminar manual (Fort Worth, Texas: Search Ministries, 1991,) 54-55.

3. Timothy Keller, *The Reason for God: Belief in an Age of Skepticism*, (New York: Dutton, 2008),xvii.

4. Timothy J. Keller, *Center Church*, (Grand Rapids: Zondervan, 2012), 115.

Chapter 12: Making the Mission Possible

1. Revelation 21:1-5
2. Cited in K.C. Hinckley, *Living Proof: A Small Group Video Series Discussion Guide*, 95.
3. Arthur Krystal, "Why Smart People Believe in God," *American Scholar* (Autumn 2001): 69.
4. Ibid, 78.
5. C. S. Lewis, *The Weight of Glory* (New York: Collier, 1980), 3–4.

Chapter 13: Launching New Believers

1. Dallas Willard, *The Spirit of the Disciplines: Understanding How God Changes Lives* (New York: Harper/San Francisco, 1990), pp 258-259.
2. 1 Cor. 3:1f; 1 John 2:13
3. Acts 9:10-17
4. Walter Larimore, M.D, *10 Essentials of Highly Healthy People* (Grand Rapids: Zondervan, 2003), pages 135-155.
5. Acts 2:41
6. 1 Thessalonians 4:9-12
7. John 4:39
8. John 9:1-11
9. Acts 11:19-21
10. 2 Corinthians 5:17; Ephesians 2:4-5
11. Romans 8:29; 2 Corinthians 3:18; Philippians 1:6; Galatians 5:22-23

Chapter 14: One Life at a Time

1. William H. McRaven, "Life Lessons from Navy SEALS Training," *The Wall Street Journal*, May 24, 2014, Section A, page 11.
2. Charles Krauthammer, *Things That Matter: Three Decades of Passions, Pastimes, and Politics*, (New York: Crown Forum, 2013), 24.
3. Cited in *John Pollock, A Man Who Changed His Times* (Burke, Va.: The Trinity Forum, 1996), 11.
4. Cited in Pollock, *A Man Who Changed His Times*, 7.
5. Matthew 4:19
6. Acts 1:8

Acknowledgments

From cover to cover, this book has been influenced by many people. Jim Petersen of the Navigators and Bill Kraftson of Search Ministries inspired us to think in a new way about our own spiritual influence. The writings of C. S. Lewis, Joe Aldridge, Rebecca Pippert, Tim Keller, and Dorothy Sayers helped to shape our philosophy.

Our friends and colleagues at the Christian Medical and Dental Associations helped us lay the foundation for this book, as we worked out the principles and applications for healthcare professionals in The Saline Solution and Grace Prescriptions conferences. We sincerely appreciate the confidence of Dr. David Stevens, Dr. Gene Rudd, Dave Bushong, Barbara Snapp, Melinda Mitchell, and the entire staff of CMDA.

We also want to thank the team at Zondervan, who first believed that *Workplace Grace* deserved to be published. Their confidence is magnified by the project's three major book awards.

For this new edition of *Workplace Grace*, we are deeply indebted to Kathy Peel for guiding edits and updates for today's readers who face new workplace challenges. We also thank Ivey Harrington Beckman, editor extraordinaire, and Amanda Battaglia, Center for Faith & Work Communications Director, for their excellent contributions.

Bill Peel: I greatly appreciate the unflagging commitment of my many colleagues in the faith-and-work movement, giving a special call-out to Marcus Goodyear, Bill Lamberth, Justin Foreman, Al Erisman, and David Gill. I am also deeply grateful for my colleagues at LeTourneau University, especially to Dr. Dale Lunsford, whose unrelenting commitment to faith and work prompted this new edition of *Workplace Grace*.

Walt Larimore: Dr. John Hartman, my partner in medical practice for more than sixteen years, deserves special thanks. John and I hammered out the principles in this book through trial and error in our medical practice in Kissimmee, Florida. Also, God has used many pastors to impact my life particularly Donald Tabb, Larry Miller, Mac Bare, Ken Hicks, Nathan Blackwell, Chris Taylor, and Bill Story.

We also wish to acknowledge the following business leaders who provided interviews for both the written and audio versions of this book: Jack Alexander, Anne Beiler, Larry Collett, Jack DeWitt, James Lindemann, Norm Miller, Merrill Oster, John Seiple, Marvin (Skip) Schoenhals, and Jose Zeilstra.

We shower praise on our wives, Kathy Peel and Barb Larimore, who enrich our lives and spur us to be our best. And heartfelt hugs go to our children, John, Joel, and James Peel and Kate and Scott Larimore, all now grown with families of their own. To be a father is an unspeakable blessing, and we have no greater joy than to see that our children are walking in the truth. Thanks for allowing us to practice our faith on and with you.

Bill Peel, Dallas, Texas

Walt Larimore, Colorado Springs, Colorado

About LeTourneau University

 **LETOURNEAU UNIVERSITY**

LeTourneau University provides a distinctly Christ-centered approach to teaching and learning.

Consistently ranked in the top tier of "America's Best Colleges," LeTourneau University serves more than 25,000 alumni and 2700 students who represent all 50 states, more than 30 countries, and 47 different denominational groups.

In addition to its residential campus in Longview, Texas, LeTourneau University offers undergraduate and graduate programs online and at educational centers in Dallas and Houston. Undergraduate, graduate, and professional programs include:

► Aeronautical Science

► Biblical Studies

► Arts and Sciences

► Business, Accounting and Economics

► Criminal Justice

► Education

► Engineering and Engineering Technology

► Health-Science

► Liberal Arts

► Nursing

► Psychology

For more information, please visit *LETU.edu*

The Center for Faith & Work

The Center for Faith & Work at LeTourneau University trains and equips Christians to see their career as a holy calling and challenges them to fulfill their role in the Great Commission as Christ's ambassadors in the workplace. The Center for Faith & Work serves…

- ▶ **Christians in the Workplace.** Online resources and live workshops help Christians connect Sunday worship with Monday work.

- ▶ **the Church.** Sermons, worship aids, and curricula help pastors prepare and deploy Christians to their workplace mission fields.

- ▶ **the Campus.** Co-curricular programs help students define their calling and develop vision for serving Christ in their professions.

Online Resource Library

Visit our online library at CenterForFaithAndWork.com to find…

- ▶ articles and essays that address workplace challenges in a post-Christian world.
- ▶ inspiring videos and interviews.
- ▶ book reviews and small-group studies.
- ▶ sermon outlines and worship ideas for church leaders.
- ▶ guidelines for building a business to the glory of God.

Conferences

Workplace Grace | Influence others for Christ in simple, non-threatening ways

Discover Your Destiny | Identify your unique giftedness and personal calling

Juggling Work And Family | Create a balanced lifestyle that fosters strong family bonds and a smoothly running home

Additional topics available. Contact us at *CFW@LETU.edu*.

About R.G. LeTourneau
1888-1969

The first half of the twentieth century was a time of both pain and prosperity, marked by two world wars and a devastating economic depression that rocked the globe. It was also a time of tremendous opportunity in America for R. G. LeTourneau, who found himself at the right place at the right time under the providence of God. With only a seventh-grade education, LeTourneau designed and manufactured earthmoving machines that helped America's military win World War II and build America's highway system after the war. He held more than 300 patents.

Humble Beginnings

Robert Gilmore LeTourneau was born on November 30, 1888. Recounting his adolescent years, his mother described him as restless, inquisitive, energetic, and ambitious. His brothers said he was fanatically determined to amount to nothing. LeTourneau himself writes, "My father's opinion of me during my first fourteen years was usually expressed in a wide selection of Bible verses aimed at describing the fate of rebellious boys like me."

At age fourteen, LeTourneau announced, "I'm a man growed." He left school and landed his first job, hauling sand for molds at Portland Ironworks. By age 30, LeTourneau had become a husband and father, but he was also in debt and unemployed. On the lookout for work, one day he repaired a farmer's tractor. Then he leveled the farmer's field to prove that the tractor was fixed. This experience became the launch pad for building a business doing what he loved to do: move dirt.

Spiritual Crisis

Confusion set in when LeTourneau's missionary sister chastised him to get serious about serving God. He felt conflicted about the work he loved and what most people believed: that "going all out for God" meant becoming "a preacher, or an evangelist, or a missionary, or what we call a full-time Christian worker." He attended a revival meeting at his church and made a commitment to give his life fully to God.

Thinking he was headed to the mission field, he sought guidance from his pastor. After they prayed together, his pastor remarked, "You know Brother LeTourneau, God needs businessmen as well as preachers and missionaries." LeTourneau responded, "All right, if that's what God wants me to be, I'll try to be His businessman." That decision established his business partnership with God, which lasted almost 60 years.

LeTourneau took the idea of being God's business partner seriously, although he thought God was getting a sorry specimen as a partner. Throughout his career and lifetime, he credited God for his success—and believed that his success made him a debtor to both God and his fellowman. This perspective prompted a lifestyle marked by extreme generosity. It also drove his commitment to do quality work, to build bigger and better machines, and to help his employees flourish spiritually and physically. He hired both Christian and non-Christian workers, and employed full-time workplace chaplains. He developed new products to keep plants open and people employed, and he took personal responsibility for any company failures.

LeTourneau's faith in his Partner also made him a risk taker, although he was careful not to presume on God's blessing. He believed, "When the Lord has a job for you to do, He'll give you the strength and the ability to do it."

His Perspective of Work

LeTourneau's ingenuity, industrious spirit, and life experiences coalesced into a simple but profound theology of work. Toward the end of his life he wrote, "When He created the world and everything in it, He didn't mean for us to stop there and say, 'God, you've done it all. There's nothing left for us to build.' He wanted us to take off from there and really build for His greater glory." LeTourneau believed the ingenuity to do that came from God. He said, "No one has ever measured the inventiveness that Christ awakens in a man's soul because it is beyond measurement."

LeTourneau recognized the theological implications of his earthly inventions. "If there is no logical explanation for my development of the digger, there's a theological one, available to all of us, including the weakest. By accepting God as your partner, there is no limit on what can be achieved. But God is no remote partner, satisfied if you go to church on Sunday and drop some religious money—the small change that goes to church—on the platter. He isn't overwhelmed if you read the Bible once in a while and obey the Golden Rule."

When he opened a plant in Peoria, Illinois, LeTourneau spoke to the Chamber of Commerce and made the following remark.

> Now I ask you, what's the use of having a religion that won't work? If I had a religion that limped along during the week, and maybe worked only on Sunday, or while you're in church, I don't think I'd be very sold on it. I think I'd turn it in on a new model that worked seven days a week, that would work when I was at church, in my home, or out at the plant. And that is what Christianity does.

His Legacy

For more than 50 years LeTourneau traveled the world and called laypeople to go to work for Jesus Christ. Many began gathering in small groups, teaching each other what it meant to follow Christ in the workplace. LeTourneau became a leading spokesperson for the lay-led, faith-and-work movement in the mid-twentieth century, laying the groundwork for today's swelling faith-and-work movement.

In 1930, LeTourneau helped launch the Christian Businessmen's Committee, which today claims 90,000 members around the world.

He believed that it was the job of Christians in business to redeem the nation. He challenged laymen to take their place alongside pastors to make faith concrete.

> The preachers can tell us that Christianity works. ... But unless we businessmen ... testify that Christianity is the driving power of our business, you'll always have doubters claiming that religion is all talk and no production.

Young people who heard LeTourneau speak often felt called to business as their path to serving God. Many of them later attended LeTourneau University, which he and his wife, Evelyn, founded in 1946 to prepare students to work and serve God.

Though LeTourneau influenced the lives of countless thousands during his lifetime, LeTourneau University could well be his greatest contribution to God's kingdom. Today, 25,000 dedicated alumni—leaders in engineering, manufacturing, business, aviation, education, and vocational ministry—know their work matters to God, and use their education and skills to impact workplaces around the world.

Although the integration of faith and work has been a consistent part of LeTourneau University's DNA since the first day of class, today the university has once again taken its place in the global faith-and-work movement. The Center of Faith & Work champions R.G. LeTourneau's faith-and-work legacy in pursuit of claiming every workplace in every nation for Christ.

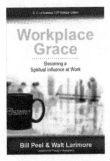

Workplace Grace Workshops

Thousands of Christians around the world have attended *Workplace Grace* Workshops and learned simple, non-threatening ways to become a spiritual influence at work. Participants learn how to…

▶ broach spiritual topics and talk about their faith in winsome ways.

▶ recognize the key role they play in God's Kingdom.

▶ build trust with skeptical coworkers and colleagues.

▶ be a witness according to their God-given design.

▶ embrace their role in the Great Commission with new confidence and enthusiasm.

What Participants Say

The best evangelism training seminar we have ever experienced. That's not hyperbole—this seminar was excellent. Larimore and Peel took the fear of evangelism away for ordinary laypeople.

—Covenant Presbyterian Church (Austin,TX)

Take advantage of this unique opportunity to prepare your people to bring Jesus to their colleagues, friends, and family.

—Woodale Church (Minneapolis, MN)

Our people were inspired and provided with simple handles for cultivating relationships with pre-Christians by serving them in Christ's love.

—Mechanicsburg Brethren in Christ Church (Mechanicsburg, PA)

Contact the Center for Faith & Work for more information about Workplace Grace Workshops.

CFW@LETU.edu

9 780989 647908